ONE I LOVE

ONE I LOVE

A DEVOTIONAL FOR COUPLES

Joy Jacobs and Ruth Dourte

Photographs by David N. Dixon

Christian Publications
Camp Hill, Pennsylvania

Photographs © 1991 David N. Dixon

Design by David N. Dixon and Stephen Fieser

Edited by Jonathan L. Graf

DEDICATION

We lovingly dedicate this book
    to our husbands, Bob and Eber
    to the Jacobs children: Rob, Rick and David
    to the Dourte children: Ray, Esther and Faithe
and to all their children and children's children
so that those who follow us
    may know and remember
    some of the things we have learned
    in our pilgrimages
        through life and relationships.

Joy Jacobs and Ruth Dourte

CONTENTS

PREFACE

At this writing Bob and Joy Jacobs had been married 23 years; Eber and Ruth Dourte had been married 46 years. Each couple has three children.

From Bob and Eber:

We have been together with Joy and Ruth in a Couples' Share and Bible Study Group for many years and have learned to know each other well.

All of us have learned new realities about men and women, common themes in marriage struggles we hadn't taken time to learn before.

And we are glad, because our marriages are now better.

Our wives have written this book, but as husbands we want to tell you a few things, too. . . .

These imaginary conversations about the life experiences of couples in the Bible remind us sometimes of conversations with our wives. At times we've been impatient while listening to all those words—and defensive while we're trying to think what to answer—but this book helps all of us want to listen more carefully to each other. It helps us want to pay attention to the feelings behind the words.

We are going to use this book with Joy and Ruth. We hope the two of you will use it together, too.

FOREWORD

This book is an imaginary visit with couples of the Bible. We observe some of their daily struggles and listen for their conversations and feel their frustrations. We identify with them, these ancient, mysterious husbands and wives. We try to put ourselves in their places and respond to their dilemmas with our own modern dilemmas.

The message of the book is this:
- *Relationships* are fragile (handle with care) and perishable (today is precious).
- *Time* is like a coin. You can spend it any way you wish, but you can spend it only once. There is no "satisfaction guaranteed" return policy.

We present this book in the hope:
- that you recognize the preciousness of your marriage and of your children.
- that you will plan as carefully for the maintenance of relationships
    —their durability and lastingness
    —the satisfaction and enjoyment they give
    —the comfort and security they provide
  as you do for your house or your car
    —regular checkups
    —regular tuneups
    —regular cleaning
    —regular loving repair and restoration.
- that you will face disturbing issues in your relationship
    —while your love is fresh and vigorous
    —as soon as you detect any anxiety.
- that children will be spared the devastation
    —of poor parenting
    —of broken marriages.

10

How to use this book:
- Read it aloud to each other! There are 31 imaginary visits with couples of the Bible—one for each day of the month.
- Use it for discussion in your family, with your friends, in groups, in Sunday school classes. Give it as a gift to newlyweds—or for couples celebrating anniversaries.

Read the Scripture story.
- Find yourself in these ancient marriage relationships. These were real people—not supersaints—with real problems and conflicts like yours and mine. The Scriptures "find me and correct me."
- The Scriptures were given
    —for our learning
    —for our comfort (endurance)
    —for our consolation (encouragement)
    —that we might have *hope!* (Romans 15:4).

Every marriage has problems.
- Problems are filled with potential
    —potential for failure
    —potential for success.

A good marriage has two good problem solvers.
- You can decide what kind of marriage you will have.
- Don't allow your commitment to rust or rot away.
- Begin now
    —to communicate
    —to plan
    —to make necessary changes.

IN THE
GARDEN OF EDEN

ADAM AND EVE

This is probably the most familiar of all Bible stories, the true story of a man and a woman living in "The Garden of Eden," a symbol of paradise, and eating "forbidden fruit," a symbol of evil.

God gave both of them dominion and authority over everything on earth. He gave them power to reproduce themselves in children. He gave them security and fellowship in their relationships with each other and with Him.

However, God retained His own dominion and authority. He declared limits. He forbade them to eat of the Tree of the Knowledge of Good and Evil.

Yet both Adam and Eve failed. Satan appeared in the disguise of a talking snake, and Adam's wife made the first mistake—entering into conversation with Satan. This opened her mind to doubts about God's authority and dominion. She ate the forbidden fruit and gave some to Adam, who ate also.

Immediately the deadly effects of the knowledge of good and evil gripped them. They now knew how wonderful *good* is and how horrible *evil* is! They tried to hide from God who easily found them and taught them an eternally painful lesson: No one can sin without hard consequences.

Read the whole story. There is mystery and *hope*: The Tree of Life!

Bible Background: Genesis 1:26–31, 2:15–25, 3:1–12.

13

EVE

FIG LEAVES, WATERGATE AND OTHER COVER-UPS

They had it all, didn't
they—
   beautiful bodies
    perfect intellect
     unscarred souls
      painless memories
       unselfish love.

But she listened to the
   serpent
and the longing of the flesh
   beguiled her
   the lust of the eyes
    entranced her
   the pride of life
    seduced her
and she sinned
and Adam with her.

Why didn't he take her hand
  and pull her from the tree?
She was made for him, his
   perfect treasure;
  why then didn't he protect
   her?

She had to make the choice
  and so did he.
She failed
  and he failed too.
They sinned together
  yet suddenly alone

and separated from their God,
  began to die that day.
Sin separates us too, my love.
The subtle serpent speaks
  appeals to eyes . . . and flesh . . .
   and pride of life.
Bites of enticing fruit
  all call for fig-leaf cover.
Please take my hand, my love.
Pray us away from strangely
  beckoning fruit.

Your wedding day whisked you breath-lessly away, all the way back to the Garden of Eden, the fairyland of happiness, of never-ending bliss. . . .

You could not see, then, that Christian marriage, a covenant of mutual sacrificial love, is such a threat to Satan's domain that he must contrive untiringly to spoil God's good thing.

Are you alert to his intention to spoil your marriage? To his clever deceptions? Are you walking with God in the garden of your life?

"For everything in the world—the cravings of sinful man, the lust of his eyes and the boasting of what he has and does—comes not from the Father, but from the world" (1 John 2:16).

14

ADAM

DIFFERENTNESS

She's beautiful, God!
  Look at her lying there
    all curled up in a ball
      smiling at a lazy dream
        that passed me by.
I lie here, wide awake,
    wanting her.

If she weren't sleeping
  she'd correct me
    if I said all this aloud.
She'd laugh and say,
  "I was not curled up in a
        ball.
    I was in the fetal position.
      Didn't you know?
  And it wasn't a lazy
        dream—
    they all have meaning,
      come from the
        subconscious.
        Don't you think?"

She'd go on talking
  as I reach out to her
    and muffle her words
      with my lips. . . .

She wants to know
  and think
    and talk
      about so many things.
Sometimes it scares me.

What was Adam to think of her? He saw their similarity—"bone of my bone, flesh of my flesh." But he also saw their differentness—he said, "She shall be called Isha, woman"—soft and delicate; he was Ish, man—strong and muscular. Later he called her Eve because she would become the mother of all human life.

Both male and female portray on earth some important aspect of the image of God—but oh, how maddeningly elusive it is sometimes to comprehend it! So we must stand in awe of it.

Are you respectful of the differentness of your spouse?

———————

"So God created man in his own image, in the image of God he created him; male and female he created them" (Genesis 1:27).

15

BANISHED FROM PARADISE

SONS OF ADAM, DAUGHTERS OF EVE

Here come those hard consequences of sin. The sweet fellowship of walking in obedience to God was gone now. Shame and blame took its place.

Eve blamed the serpent, and Adam blamed Eve. But God accepted no excuses and pronounced upon each the deadly effects of their sin.

Eve and her daughters suffer pain and confusion in their relationships to their husbands and in the bearing and rearing of children.

Adam and his sons find the work of caring for earth's resources difficult and bitter. The ground which Adam tilled reminded him daily of his impending death—"You are dust, and to dust you must return."

The pleasure of their togetherness and their work was tainted with painful memories and regret.

But—God gave them help and *hope*. He spared them from living forever in sin and placed an angel to guard the way to the Tree of Life.

God promised Satan's defeat and humanity's ultimate victory. If people will now live God's way, instead of their own way, they *will* eat of the Tree of Life—eternal life!

You will want to read the *whole* Bible to find out how!

Bible Background: Genesis 3:8–24, 4:1–17.

17

DAUGHTERS OF EVE

Where has it gone
—my confidence—
the gift I didn't know I had
until I lost it?

Why do I feel
so suddenly bereft of beauty
so large with yet another
baby
afraid of terrible tearing
pain
and feeling so alone?

And when I ask him where
he's been
does he avoid my questions
evade my searching eyes
become annoyed because I
ask?

I feel so unacceptable
somehow
where I once felt so
cherished
valued
loved.

He's not accountable to me.
It seems he does just as he
pleases.
Is he accountable to You?
I hope so, God.
How else will we survive?

Perhaps it's just the awkwardness
that makes me feel this way.
You gave me this sweet privilege
and I know
You love me as I am—
huge, hurting, heavy
in mind as well as body.

And when the child is born
the joy will come.

How vulnerable, how unable to fully protect or provide for herself the female of the species is when she carries or gives birth to her young!

She seems to go on a long journey inside herself, a realm where mystery and magic reign, where God creates anew another "man" or "woman" in the cavity of her humanness. And God said, "It is not good to be alone."

Are you taking that journey together?

———————————

"We know that the whole creation has been groaning as in the pains of childbirth right up to the present time"" Romans 8:27).

SONS OF ADAM

ACCOUNTABILITY

You could have warned
me, God,
  that she would change like
    this!
Oh, not her figure
  she's so concerned about—
    it's her emotions
      that drive me up the
        wall!
No one prepared me!
  Well, I guess my mother
    tried.

Hey, come to think of it,
  Adam had it worse, poor
    guy!
No one at all to warn him
    give him advice
    chasten him when
      needed.
He had to be accountable to
  You.

Some days
  I find that very hard—
    to be accountable to You
      and her.
You know I love her
  but sometimes
    responsibilities pile up
      and I want out.
        There, that's the truth!

Those carefree days
    of cruisin' with the guys. . . .
Hey, that's another thing poor Adam
    missed!
  I guess it's worse for her
  carrying her responsibility
    —ours, I mean—
      with her day and night.

Please help me, God.
  Please grow me up.
    Teach me accountability.
      I need to learn.

Every man began his life carried and cared for by a woman. Many men never come full cycle to that maturity that makes them able and willing to watch over and care for women and children, in much the same way that they were once watched over and cared for by a woman.

Daughters simply identify with mother. Sons must differentiate from her and learn to love in ways that do not come so naturally. Are you learning such "watchcare" love?

"When I was a child . . . I reasoned like a child. When I became a man, I put childish ways behind me" (1 Corinthians 13:11).

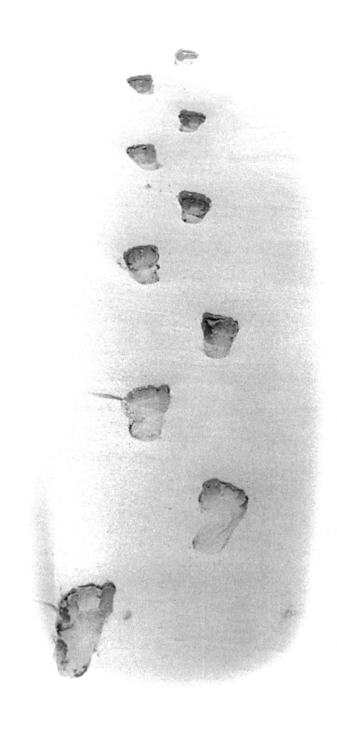

A MAN WHO DID NOT DIE

MR. AND MRS. ENOCH

When Enoch was 65 years old his little son Methuselah was born. It is specifically stated that "after he became the father of Methuselah, Enoch walked with God for 300 years and had other sons and daughters." Altogether, Enoch lived 365 years.

Did the awesomeness, the responsibility of the birth of his firstborn make such an impact on Enoch that it caused him to take God seriously for the first time in his life?

He walked with God so closely that he did not experience death. He could not be found because God had taken him away. Before his disappearance he was commended as one who pleased God.

Did his life begin a righteous line? His son Methuselah was the grandfather of Noah. When Noah was born, his father Lamech said of him, "He will comfort us in the labor and painful toil of our hands."

Bible Background: Genesis 5:21–29, Hebrews 11:5.

21

ENOCH

Enoch walked with God.
It's said he pleased God.
And then one day
he was no more.

After 365 years
—years, not days—
of walking with God
Enoch could not be
found.

God had taken him away.

He was walking with God—
a few steps higher.

And his son Methuselah
lived 669 more years
to tell the story
of a dad
who walked with God.

When you are an old man, an old woman, sitting in your rocking chair, feeble and frail, the zeal and fire of former years almost gone . . . what will matter then?

What will your children remember about you? Will they gather around you with tenderness and respect, nourishing the flickering flame of your life?

Will money or property or degrees or trophies warm your heart when the breath of death blows cold on your body?

Will you be thinking in your heart, "I'm glad I did . . ." rather than "I wish I had . . ."?

"I consider everything a loss compared to the surpassing greatness of knowing Christ Jesus my Lord, for whose sake I have lost all things. . . . I want to know Christ and the power of his resurrection and the fellowship of sharing in his sufferings, becoming like him in his death, and so, somehow, to attain to the resurrection from the dead" (Philippians 3:8, 10–11).

MRS. ENOCH

WALKING TOGETHER

At first glance I thought,
Wouldn't it be wonderful
  to love a man
    who walked with God?

On second thought . . .
  if he walked with God
    would he have time
      to walk with me?

I think so.

After all, God walked in the
    Garden
  in the cool of the day
    with both Adam and Eve
  before they learned to hide
  from His presence.

Some people sincerely fear that a close walk with God will surely lead into a bleak and dreary land, into duty without joy, into poverty without provision, into suffering without solace.

They cannot believe that walking with God could enrich human relationships as well.

If you walk with God He will whisper, "Husbands, love your wives as Christ loved . . ." and "Beloved, love one another as I have loved you."

Love is safe in only one place in the whole world—in the very center of God's will, guided and guarded by His Spirit.

Are you both walking there?

———

"I pray also for those who will believe in me . . . that all of them may be one, Father, just as you are in me and I am in you. May they also be in us so that the world may believe that you have sent me" (John 17:20–21).

GOOD MORNING. . .

MR. AND MRS. NOAH

How are you today? We hear that you are in a momentous undertaking, and all the neighbors are talking about it. Please explain."

"Well," said Mr. Noah, "I have tried to please God all of my 500 years, even though the wickedness all around makes it very hard. Even God is sorry He made people. So, He told me to build this huge boat to save my family and the animal kingdom from being completely wiped out. Maybe my father Lamech had some kind of vision when he named me.

"But people think we are crazy because, until now, it has never even rained. I am already an old man and have worked on this boat over a hundred years. God told me exactly how to build it, how to gather the animals and provide food for our voyage.

"However, my fellowship with God all of my life has given me absolute trust and faith. Nothing could be worse than giving up and giving in to all of this unspeakable wickedness and violence in our world.

"Won't you change your mind and join my family in God's plan to save us?"

Bible Background: Genesis 5–8, 9:1–17.

25

MRS. NOAH

THE LIFE OF A ZOOKEEPER'S WIFE

Some days my husband seems
  so totally immersed in his
    career.
But you know, Lord, I was
    thinking today
of how tired Noah's wife
    must have gotten
of hearing about the ark
and of watching her
    husband
spend every spare minute
    working on it.
Was she thankful that
  after Noah was already an
    old man
    God sent three sons
      to help him build the
      ark?
She probably wasn't too
    young either!

When the boys grew up
  she must have watched all
    four men
    nailing, sawing, pounding
    nailing, sawing, pounding
    nailing, sawing, pounding
  then rounding up those
    animals
    to join the floating zoo
  then feeding, tending,
    watering
    a seasick, frightened zoo.

I'm glad I'm not Mrs. Noah.
  I'd rather be me
    with my busy husband
    and just one dog
      just one cat
    and two guinea pigs—
      last time I looked.

Perhaps Mrs. Noah was very lonely at times!

"Togetherness" in marriage is more a matter of understanding and support, a unity of heart and mind and purpose, than of physical proximity.

Such unity rests on the foundation of deep sharing—a kind of emotional foreplay and verbal intercourse—which is the background music for satisfying partnership. Such intimacy produces an ecstasy which far surpasses and outlasts mere physical union.

Have you experienced the rewards of this true and total oneness?

"Jesus prayed to His Father, 'I have given them the glory that you gave me, that they may be one as we are one: I in them and you in me' " (John 17:22–23a).

NOAH

How did he do it, Lord?
How did he stand up
to all the ridicule
the neighbors must
have heaped on him?
Did they mock him?
laugh at him?
complain about the
noise?
the smell of the
animals?
the pollution?
After all, there had never
been a flood before.
How *could* they
understand?

I'm not that strong, Lord.
I find it hard
to hold up under
pressure at work
to even bow my head at
lunch
to keep from listening
and laughing at dirty
jokes
to stand up for what I
believe.

Please give me Noah's courage, Lord,
to buck a doubting world current
and stay afloat,
family intact.

Until I understood better, it seemed unfair that God had made the road to life narrow. Then I realized that Jesus was simply stating a fact: Any path or road is narrow because only a few people walk on it.

Sometimes it's lonely on the narrow road to life because few people, as Jesus said, find it.

Some people see only the difficulties on the seldom-used road and are afraid to walk there. But Jesus said it will lead to life, while the well-travelled road will lead to destruction.

Will the two of you decide to walk together, never alone, on the safe path of God's good will for you?

"Enter through the narrow gate. For wide is the gate and broad is the road that leads to destruction, and many enter through it. But small is the gate and narrow the road that leads to life, and only a few find it" (Matthew 7:13–14).

THE SIN OF SELF-PROTECTION

ABRAHAM AND SARAH

This ancient couple had lived through a lot of hard things since they left their homeland, wandering from one place to another, always trying to understand if this was where God wanted them.

There was famine that led Abram with Sarai to Egypt and his first lie. There were problems because of the wealth he and Lot had accumulated and a parting of their ways. There were border raids, kidnappings, battles and victories.

Many times Abram did things his own way, but always he returned to his worship of God. God eventually changed their names to Abraham and Sarah. He renewed His promise to make of Abraham a great nation by giving him a son in his old age.

After entertaining heavenly visitors and interceding with God for Lot's deliverance from Sodom, Abraham moved again and lied a second time to another ruler, saying, "This beautiful woman Sarah is my sister." It was a half-truth, a half-lie, since she was a half sister, but in each case the rulers discovered the lie and still spared Abraham. Why did pagan kings have that much respect for marriage?

Why was Abraham so self-protective, so fearful of being killed because he was married to Sarah?

Bible Background: Genesis 12:10–20, 20:1–18, Hebrews 11:8–12, 1 Peter 3:1–6.

29

ABRAHAM

A MAN OF FAITH

It's really strange, Lord,
  that a man like Abraham
    the "father of many
      nations"
    would lie
  just to save his skin.

Worse than that,
  in the process
    he endangered the life
      of his wife.
I can just imagine
  my wife's reaction
    to assignment to a harem
      for just one hour!

Worst of all,
  years later
    his son Isaac
      followed in his father's
        footsteps.
Wow!
Guess I'd better watch where
    I walk.

Please guide me, Lord,
  as You guided Abraham—
    when he was listening.

P.S. It's good to know that
    You forgive.

Is walking by faith guaranteed to keep you from ever failing or falling? Hardly. Is faith then blind? No!

Faith is walking in all the light you have at the present time, trusting that because of your obedience, God will then show you the next step. Abraham, the father of faith, "went out not knowing" how, when or where God would fulfill His promise.

When Abraham followed his own understanding, he was in trouble. But he always got back on track, and God blessed him.

God will also bless your obedience. What is He telling you to do now—together?

"Do not lie to each other, since you have taken off your old self with its practices and have put on the new self, which is being renewed in knowledge in the image of its Creator" (Colossians 3:9–10).

SARAH

MY LORD. . .

It's very hard for me to see
  how the story of old
    Abraham
  and his ancient wife, Sarah,
    had anything to do with
      us.
She called him "lord"—
  imagine that!
If I ever tried to say
  "my lord" to you, my love,
    I'd laugh!
    We'd laugh together.
You'd like it, wouldn't you,
    though?

"My lord". . . as you lie there
    asleep,
  so strong, yet so vulnerable,
I realize you are just a boy—
  a big one, but a boy.
You love to play those games
  that sometimes seem so
    childish. . .
    I guess I'm growing up.
I wonder . . . did my mother
  feel this same way toward
    my dad
    when they were young?
My daddy seems so sure of
    things—
  but was he always?

Did she wonder . . .
  could she trust his
    judgment?
  rely on his decisions?
  accept his choices?

God . . . is that why You called Sarah
    beautiful
  because she trusted You
    even when her husband made
      mistakes
  and, most of all, forgave him?

Well, what about the behavior of wives? The Bible says, "Wives, submit to your husbands as to the Lord." Yes, she must yield to all of her husband's efforts to care for her in Christlike ways: "Husbands, love your wives, just as Christ loved the church and gave himself up for her to make her holy."

Christian marriage does not have a boss and a servant. It has two servants. Nothing in all the world was so submissive as the love of Jesus.

Love and submission are two sides of one coin—of two becoming one.

Are you submitting to one another out of reverence for Christ?

"You are [Sarah's] daughters if you do what is right and do not give way to fear" (1 Peter 3:6b).

PERILS OF PROSPERITY

MR. AND MRS. LOT

Wealthy Lot and Uncle Abram could no longer live or travel together. Their herds of livestock were too large and the herdsmen were quarreling. So Abram allowed Lot to choose for himself the well-watered plain of Jordan, where he became a part of the city life of Sodom.

Meanwhile Abram lived in the hill country and without bitterness rescued his greedy nephew, Lot, from raiding rulers. Later he pled with God in prayer to save Lot from the predicted destruction of wicked Sodom.

God answered Abram's prayer by sending two angels who had to grab Lot's family and forcibly lead them to safety. Even then Lot argued for the privilege of fleeing to a nearby town instead of to the mountains as he was commanded to do.

But it was too close. When Lot's wife disobeyed the angels' command not to even look back toward Sodom, she became a pillar of salt, as burning sulfur rained down on the cities of Sodom and Gomorrah.

Even Jesus said, "Remember Lot's wife."

Bible background: Genesis 13:5–11, 19:1–29, Luke 17:28–36.

33

MRS. LOT

THE BACKWARD LOOK

She couldn't face a new day
  a new home
    a new life with her hus-
      band.

She looked back
  to the past
    and looked back again.
She fell behind
  and Sodom's explosion
    reached out and covered
      her
      with its corruption.
  Her backward look
    solidified into salt
      for all posterity to see.
Sadly enough
  in their actions
    her daughters continued
      her backward look.

She married a prosperous, clever man who knew a good deal when he saw it. And perhaps Lot gave her everything she wanted.

Perhaps she began to see her husband as a money tree, whose limbs she systematically picked bare of its dangling fruit. Then she ungraciously sent him out the door to "grow" some more . . . .

Husbands or wives may lay down their lives, at work or at home, inch by inch, day by day, trying desperately to gain some recognition, some respect, some comfort and encouragement—but it so seldom comes.

The emptiness digs itself deeper and deeper, and the lonely cries for love echo back from the hollow walls of the marketplace and the prison walls of a house called home.

Do you live like you really understand that the thirst of the human soul for love can never be satisfied with things money can buy?

"For the love of money is a root of all kinds of evil. Some people, eager for money, have wandered from the faith and pierced themselves with many griefs" (1 Timothy 6:10).

LOT

NEEDS . . . AND WANTS

I tried to find the perfect spot
  in just the right location
    in suburbia—
  but is it good enough?

We need . . . she says.
  The children need. . . .
    That's all I ever hear!
  She's never satisfied.
  She doesn't know the
        difference
    between our needs and
        wants.
  She doesn't recognize that
        there
    are other kinds of needs.

Some days I wonder . . .
  am I just a money tree
    my limbs amputated
      by each storm of desire
        for something new?

Who nurtures the tree of my life? Materialism is as old as the human race—this serving the gods of gold and wood and stone, the gods of money and property and power.

When a man's business succeeds too well, he may no longer really own it; the business will own him. It no longer serves him; he serves the business. He becomes a slave to his own success. He is no longer free to choose what is best for himself, for his family. He is walled in.

If and when the time comes that he is forced to leave his "Sodom," as Lot found necessary, he may find it almost impossible. And its climate has taken its toll on his family's spiritual health.

Will you allow some earthly enterprise to become your slavemaster? To destroy your family life?

"The worries of this life and the deceitfulness of wealth choke [the Word], making it unfruitful" (Matthew 13:22b).

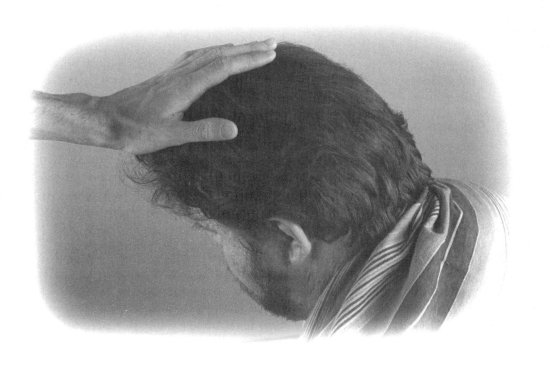

A SCENE IN THE LIFE OF ABRAHAM'S SON

ISAAC AND REBECCA

Isaac is now old and senile. His wife, Rebecca, and his twin sons, Esau and Jacob, are competing for the power that their father's dying blessing and his wealth will give them.

Mother Rebecca devises a plan to deceive Isaac into giving his blessing to her favorite son, Jacob, rather than to Esau, the firstborn twin.

The scheme succeeds, but the cheated Esau plots in his heart to kill his brother Jacob, so Rebecca urges Isaac to send Jacob away to her home country to find a wife.

Esau, trying not to be disadvantaged a second time, also chooses to marry one of Abraham's descendants, a daughter of Ishmael. It is one more effort to gain his parents' favor.

This account is full of intrigue and peril to lives and to family relationships, all because a wife allowed her son to be more important to her than her loyalty to her husband.

Bible Background: Genesis 27:1–46, 28:1–9.

ISAAC

STRONG AND SILENT

Lord . . . it's me again.
I feel like I'm complaining
  and I don't really mean it
    that way.
But sometimes
  I just don't know
    what she wants from
    me.
Back then . . . I thought she
  liked
  the strong, silent type.
It seemed like I could take
    her in my arms
  and everything would be
    all right.

But that was back then
  when she had all her
    friends to talk to.
Now she depends on me
  for adult conversation
    and, to be honest, Lord
  when I come home from
    work
    I just don't feel like
    talking.
  I need a break.

Guess that's where the
    problems start
  for lots of people. . . .
It's hard to think of her needs
  before your own.

Communication can be difficult at
    times.
It's work.

Lord . . . help me work as hard at home
  as I do at my job
    even when I'm tired.
Please help her try
  to understand me, too,
    even when I can't explain
    the way I feel.

Silence is like a frozen pond, hiding from view the pulsating life within.

Communication is like a flowing stream, or a sparkling spring, exposing itself to light and air in order to purify whatever is within.

Two streams of life in marriage may converge and mingle all together, not conspicuously aware of how each is enlarged and enriched by the other. So each of you becomes a fuller, freer self.

Communication is the major task of love. Are you making verbal sharing a priority in your marriage?

"Do not let any unwholesome talk come out of your mouths, but only what is helpful for building others up according to their needs, that it may benefit those who listen" (Ephesians 4:29).

REBECCA

THE TRIANGLE

I've seen it happen to other
couples.

They started out like us,
   so much in love
but, year by year, the barriers
      grew
   between them—
husbands married to their
      businesses,
wives whose worlds revolved
      around their
      children—
no time or love left for
      each other.

Rebecca loved her Isaac once
   —perhaps until he lied.
Respect was gone
   with love not far behind.
She zeroed in on Jacob
   and he became her all
   and she taught him to lie
      —strange ironies of life!

Isaac preferred Esau.
His "taste for game"
   involved him in a game
     of treachery and deceit
   planned, engineered and
      carried through
   by his own wife.

When did their love begin to die?
   with just one lie?
and who stopped talking first?
   and whose sin was the worst?

Three laws of holy, happy wedlock:
Leave your father and mother; cleave to
your wife; become one flesh.

What does "cleave" mean? It means
cemented or glued. Do not permit one
thing to come between the two of you:
your parents, your children, your job,
your friends or your leisure-time
activities.

Even a child can usurp first place in a
family and put spouse in second place.
That hurts everyone, including the child.

Who holds first place in your heart
and in your home?

---

*"Speaking the truth in love, we will in all
things grow up into him who is the Head,
that is, Christ"* (Ephesians 4:15).

MEMORIES OF ROMANCE

JACOB AND RACHEL

Jacob obeyed his father's command not to marry a pagan wife and went to the land where his mother's people lived.

There he met Rachel, his cousin, tending sheep. He kissed her and wept aloud and was warmly welcomed by his uncle Laban.

Laban offered Jacob a job and asked what wages he wanted. Jacob looked at beautiful Rachel and said, "I will serve you seven years for Rachel." Laban agreed, and it is well remembered that "Jacob served seven years to get Rachel, but they seemed like only a few days to him because of his love for her."

It seems, however, that deception ran in the family. For according to custom, the wife was brought to the husband by her father at night after the wedding feast. And when Jacob awoke in the morning, he discovered he had consummated a marriage to Leah, Rachel's older sister.

Jacob was dismayed, but Laban explained that, in his country, older sisters must marry before younger ones.

Jacob then served Laban another seven years for Rachel and loved her more than Leah.

Think how far this man went to prove his wife's worth!

Bible Background: Genesis 29:1–35, 30:1–2.

41

JACOB

WAITING

Sometimes, in the pure passion
　of our togetherness,
I think of Jacob waiting for
　　　Rachel
　—seven years.
I marvel at the man's
　　　restraint,
　self-discipline.
And then to think
　it was not Rachel in his bed
　his wedding night!
I think I would have killed
　my father-in-law
but times were different then.

There are so many times
　I want to tell you
　　how much I love you,
times when I see you in a
　　　crowd
　and I can hardly wait
　　to take you home
　　to have you to myself
　　　again.

So often, though,
　the words stick in my
　　　throat.
　They sound so trite,
　　so awkward.

But please believe me,
　I *would* work seven years for you
　　if that is what it took.
Fourteen, you ask?
　Now that's a different story!

How long, how devotedly could we love if there was no payoff, no personal benefits to be weighed or measured in time and space? No sexual recompense or gratification for the craving within the human heart and body?

　Waiting was so difficult before marriage. Now, waiting for anything seems unnecessary. Wait for what?

　Wait, in order to give rather than to receive. Do not withhold what is in your power to give. Jesus said that if you give generously you will receive more than you gave.

　Are you learning the rewards of waiting?

"All night long on my bed I looked for the one my heart loves; . . . I will search for the one my heart loves" (Song of Songs 3:1–2).

42

RACHEL

WATCHING

Today I caught you watch-
ing that waitress
   —the pretty one.
I wasn't prepared for the
         feelings
    that swept over me
       rejection
       jealousy
       anger
       inferiority.
I felt like Leah, the sister
       who was plain.

Then suddenly you looked at
       me and smiled.
You said,
   "To think I almost asked
       her out!
   That was before I met *you*."
And then I felt like Rachel!

Sometimes at night
   when I can't sleep
     I lie there watching you,
         my Jacob,
       loving you,
   grateful that I'm Rachel
     but sometimes
         feeling just a little sorry
             for Leah
           who never knew her
             husband's love.

I'm glad God gave her sons.

Jealousy may be very destructive, but its roots go deep into the soil of love. Jealousy can be right and good.

God Himself is a jealous God. He portrays His relationship to His people as that of a husband to a wife and does everything He can to protect His people and nurture their love for Him alone.

We must be careful never to give to other persons the time and attention that rightfully belong to our spouse or our children, nor claim for ourselves time and attention that belong to our family members.

Are you protecting your love for each other?

"Love is as strong as death, its jealousy unyielding as the grave" (Song of Songs 8:6b). *"I, the Lord your God, am a jealous God"* (Exodus 20:5b).

43

HMM! A FAMOUS COUPLE, BUT NOT MAN AND WIFE

JOSEPH AND MRS. POTIPHAR

Joseph, one of Jacob's 12 sons, was sold as a slave by his jealous older brothers and taken to Egypt. There he distinguished himself in the service of a man named Potiphar, a captain of the Pharaoh's guard, and became overseer of Potiphar's house and all of his possessions.

There in his master's house, the handsome, young Joseph faced an awesome challenge to his manhood. Potiphar's wife urged Joseph day after day to go to bed with her. He resolutely refused to do so, but she would not give up.

One day when both were alone in the house, she grabbed onto Joseph's clothing and tried to pull him into bed, but he left his garment in her hand and ran out of the house.

Angry at one more refusal, she screamed until servants came. She claimed that Joseph attacked her and that she had grabbed his garment as evidence.

Potiphar believed his wife's story and put Joseph into prison. However, Joseph's noble character was verified even in prison, where he soon became overseer of all of the prisoners.

What a man he was!

Bible Background: Genesis 37:1–28, 39:1–23.

45

MRS. POTIPHAR

THE STRANGER IN MY MIND

I wonder if Potiphar's wife
looked like
   the woman I saw in the
      grocery store—
   the one who didn't look
      like
      she should be grocery
         shopping.
She looked more
   like one of the magazine
      covers
      at the checkout
         counters.
But you know, Lord, I'm
      beginning to realize
that Potiphar's wife could
      look like *me*
   those days when I grow
      tired
      of the monotony of life
         and dream of that
         stranger
         —"Oh, faithless
         heart!"—
The "stranger" may be dark-
      haired
   or tall and blonde
      maybe thin, maybe mus-
         cular
   but always he is sensitive
      to my needs
   and always he has those
      eyes
      that search my soul
and bring out the poetry in me.
My husband can't compete with the
      stranger
   because, unlike Joseph,
   the stranger doesn't have a name
      —he isn't real—
   and yet I judge my husband against
      him
      in the courtroom of my mind.
Forgive me, Lord,
   for that first step toward sin.

Comparison is a venture into
dangerous territory where imagination
reigns. Fantasy can enrich a routine life
and foster growth toward good goals,
but fantasy can also seduce you, confuse
you and reduce a good relationship to
disillusionment.

Don't neglect the person God gave
you while you dream of the "right person" for you. Beware! Be on guard for
the affair! The idea begins so innocent-
ly—perhaps while watching television—
but it is a hidden snare set by Satan to
capture you.

Are you appreciating the good
qualities of the mate you have?

*"The heart is deceitful above all things
and beyond cure. Who can understand
it?" (Jeremiah 17:9).*

46

JOSEPH

TEMPTATION

Oh, God, how close I
came
   to staying with her!
Her eager eyes searched mine
   for signs of lust
      —God, keep them pure!
Her eager hands reached out
   to feel and touch
      —God, keep me steady!
She was ready
   willing
     very able.

Oh, God, how close I came
   to staying with her
   to giving up all I value
   to betraying all I love.

You are the only one who
      knows
   how close I came.

Temptation is temptation only if it's something you really would like to do. Otherwise you would not give it a second thought or feel the pull of it.

Jesus was tempted in every way just as we are. He had every normal human desire, but He did not sin. He could say *no* to human desire and do God's will instead.

So temptation is not a sin; *yielding* is sin. Take the way of escape; use Scripture, prayer, obedience and accountability to a caring friend.

With whom do you honestly share your struggles?

"Can a man walk on hot coals without his feet being scorched? So is he who sleeps with another man's wife; no man who touches her will go unpunished. . . . A man who commits adultery lacks judgment; whoever does so destroys himself" (Proverbs 6:28–29, 32).

47

THE IMPORTANCE OF ONE SLAVE'S LIFE

AMRAM AND JOCHEBED

As a result of Joseph's prominence in Egypt and because of severe famine, his entire family and clan eventually moved there. However, after Joseph's death, a new king, fearing the increasingly strong and populous Israelites, decided to enslave them. He hoped to weaken them and wipe out their race.

Thus every male child born to the Israelite slaves was to be killed by Egyptian midwives. But the midwives feared the Lord and therefore did not comply. So Pharaoh commanded all the people to throw Hebrew sons into the Nile River.

Amram and Jochebed hid their son for three months before she decided to make a waterproof basket for the baby, to hide him in the bulrushes along the Nile. Then she sent his sister Miriam to watch what might happen.

Miracle of miracles! The king's own daughter saw the crying baby and pitied him. At that moment little Miriam appeared and offered to find a nurse for the baby.

Guess who Miriam found! The baby's mother, of course, who was then paid by the princess to nurse him until he was old enough to be adopted as the son of the Pharaoh's daughter.

It was the princess herself who named this boy Moses, because she "drew him out of the water."

Bible Background: Exodus 1:6–22 and 2:1–10.

49

AMRAM

TRUSTING

How did Amram feel
about trusting his wife
to do right
with his son
in her handmade
basket?

After all, anything could
have happened
to a basket in the bulrushes
of the Nile—
a summer thunderstorm
a sudden flood
a swift downcurrent!
Man-eating crocodiles
would find it
bite-size.

Put *my* son in a basket
and float him down the
river?
Jochebed! Think
logically!

Why do we speak of "women's intuition"? Do men have it too? Can it be trusted, this intangible, unprovable "hunch" or nudge?

Probably not all by itself, but women tend to have a natural kind of inwardness, an awareness of invisible working and moving that often defies all logic. Women are often more sensitive to the realm of spiritual reality, the importance of faith, which is being sure of what we hope for and certain of what we do not see.

We must test all leadings, however, by both God's Word and counsel.

Do you respectfully consider each other's leadings and longings?

"The man without the Spirit does not accept the things that come from the Spirit of God, for they are foolishness to him, and he cannot understand them, because they are spiritually discerned" (1 Corinthians 2:14).

JOCHEBED

LETTING GO

Lord, I ask for Jochebed's
ability to let go
   when my children come to
     the point
   where that becomes a
     necessity.

That time came early for
     baby Moses
   —basket-boating in the
     bulrushes—
   but Jochebed let him go
   handed her son to
     heathen royalty
   because she trusted You
   to bring him through—
     not necessarily back
     to her.

Was she still alive
   when Moses left Egypt
     at age 40?
Was she still alive
   when he returned to Egypt
     40 years later?
     Probably not.

Jochebed probably died
     trusting You
   to "bring it to pass."

Lord, I need that kind of
     quiet faith.

Mothers seem to have an "emotional umbilical cord" to their children, which is never completely severed. How can you stop caring about the fruit of your womb? How can bonding become unbound? How can the pain of the empty nest, worse than the pain of the empty womb, be borne?

It can be borne only if my child is now carried "in the womb" of God. Only if I know I have done my own part of God's will in bringing a "new birth" to pass, can I bear it.

Are you preparing now for a healthy letting go of the children God has placed in your care?

———

"By faith Moses' parents hid him for three months after he was born, because they saw he was no ordinary child, and they were not afraid of the king's edict. By faith Moses . . . regarded disgrace for the sake of Christ as of greater value than the treasures of Egypt, because he was looking ahead to his reward" (Hebrews 11:23–26).

51

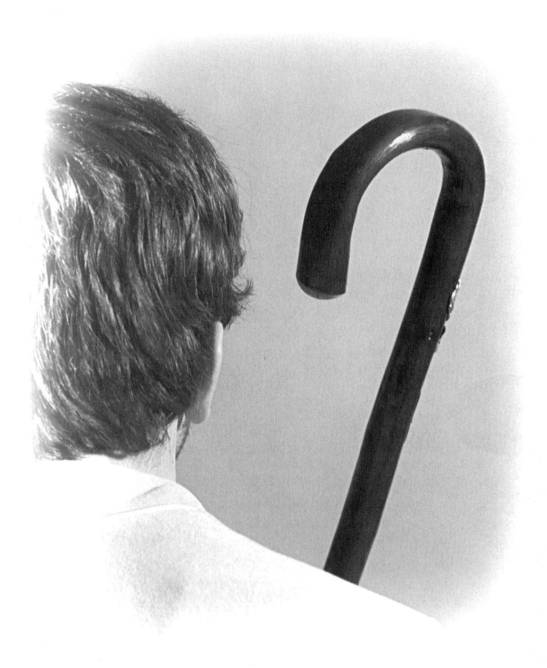

A MARRIAGE UNDER STRESS IN EXILE

MOSES AND ZIPPORAH

When Moses grew up as the son of Pharaoh's daughter, he went out to his people, the slaves, and looked on their burdens.

One day he killed an Egyptian who was beating a Hebrew. When he learned that the deed was known, he fled for his life to the land of Midian.

There he married Zipporah, one of seven daughters of the priest of Midian, and they had two sons.

In the meantime, the reigning king of Egypt died.

God appeared to Moses out of a burning bush, while he was shepherding his father-in-law's flock, and called him to go back to Egypt and deliver his people from their slavery.

God made many promises and demonstrations of His power and presence to a very fearful and doubting Moses. Eventually he and his little family began the long journey back to Egypt.

During a troubled night, while Moses was struggling with the weight of God's call, Zipporah impatiently or desperately performed the circumcision of their son and threw the foreskin at Moses' feet, thus fulfilling a neglected aspect of their obedience to God.

She then returned with her sons to her father's house until after Moses and Aaron brought the Hebrews out of Egypt.

Bible Background: Exodus 2:11–23, 3:1–12, 4:18–26, 18:1–18.

53

ZIPPORAH

CONFLICT

Lord, I see that even
Moses and his wife
   had fights.
      In fact, it seems she went
         back home
         after one of them
            and didn't see Moses
            again
               for quite some time.
Sometimes I feel like going
         home too, Lord,
      after an argument.
         Would it solve anything,
         Lord?
         I doubt it.
It's just that I feel so hurt
   and I want to be a little girl
      again
      and go home and cry
      and have Mom say:
   "You'll feel better in the
         morning, honey."

Now *I* have to be Mom
   and I'm just too tired
   and I feel so
         unappreciated.

Mom must have felt this way
         sometimes too
   but she kept right on being
         Mom.
      Mom, have I ever told you
         how much I love you?

Instead of throwing a pity party for
      myself,
   maybe I'll write you a letter, Mom,
      and tell you.

Thanks, God, for showing me
   how much I owe the people in my
      life.
Help me not to continue
   to take them for granted
      as I have
         for so much of my life.

When you are suffering from fear or failure or confusion, you need to feel the comfort and security of love.

Conflict ripens and sharpens when we do not respectfully consider all the thoughts and feelings of another person. It hurts to be turned off when you need to be turned on.

You need to explore the land of your hurts and your hopes, your weaknesses and your wishes, with someone who truly loves you. Be sure to make a place for feelings.

Are you learning to convert conflict into contentment?

"God said, 'As a mother comforts her child, so will I comfort you' " (Isaiah 66:13a).

54

MOSES

It's interesting to see the
reason
   why Moses and his wife
     had that big argument
       along the road to Egypt.

Moses, the great leader,
   wasn't doing the leading
     spiritually
      at home
        in his own family.

He was supposed to
      circumcise his son
  and didn't
  so his wife had to.

To think a man like Moses
   had the same problems
     with spiritual leadership
      that I do!

And yet God used him
   after He taught him
     a lesson he never forgot.
   He almost died
     for his lack of obedience.

I'm glad
   You're the God
     of the second chance.

How does a husband practice Christlike headship? How did Christ love the church? Just like a good shepherd cares for his sheep.

Jesus takes responsibility for our safety and our nourishment. He said He is the Light of the World, the Bread of Life, the Living Water, the Good Shepherd giving His life for the sheep. He leads us into green pastures, beside still waters. He comforts and guides us. Psalm 23 sounds like Ephesians 5.

Some husbands "use" their wives instead of "saving" them or comforting and protecting them. A good shepherd-husband leads his family to safety and sustenance even if it means giving his own life.

How do you practice such headship and submission?

"Husbands, in the same way be considerate as you live with your wives, and treat them with respect as the weaker partner and as heirs with you of the gracious gift of life, so that nothing will hinder your prayers" (1 Peter 3:7).

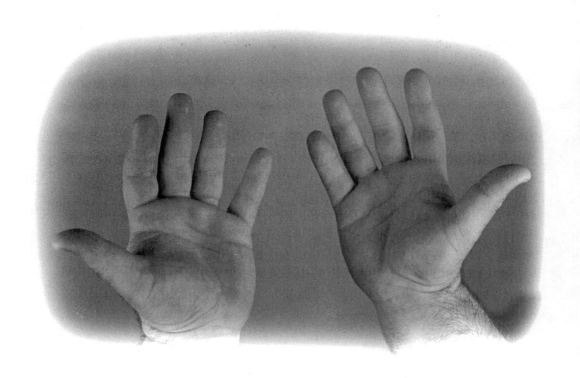

PHYSICAL AND EMOTIONAL PROBLEMS

MR. AND MRS. JOB

Job was a man of extraordinary character and wealth. He was blameless and upright. He feared God and resisted evil. He was the greatest man of his time in his country.

His seven sons had a feast every day, taking turns at each of their houses and always inviting their three sisters. How they enjoyed being together!

Job carried a daily concern for his children. He called them together every morning for family worship and confession of any sins, either in deed or thought.

Then tragedy struck, coming by the hand of Satan and with God's permission, as a test of Job's integrity and the genuineness of his faith in God.

Bands of raiders stole his oxen and camels and killed his servants. Wind and fire destroyed all of his property and killed all of his children.

Job, in agony of his soul, mourned, yet worshiped and blessed the Lord. He did not blame God or complain.

Satan then asked God's permission to afflict Job's body, and he suffered terrible sores from head to foot.

In this extremity of loss and pain, Job's wife could not suggest any cure except death by blasphemy. She said, "Curse God and die!" She could think of no way to help or comfort her husband.

Nonetheless he maintained his steadfast faith in God.

Bible Background: Job 1:1–22, 2:1–10.

57

MRS. JOB

"FOR BETTER OR WORSE . . ."

It's so easy for me, Lord,
  to notice the negativity
    of Job's wife.
It's so easy for me
  to condemn her
    for her lack of
      supportiveness.
It's so easy for me
  to feel self-righteous,
    to boast quietly:
    "I'd never say something
      like that!"

But I've never lost all my
    children
    my possessions
    my employees.
Life hasn't reduced my
    husband
  to a sore-encrusted beggar
    sitting on an ash heap
      head in hands.

I know the end of the story.
  Job's wife didn't.

I, Mary, take thee, John, to be my wedded husband, to have and to hold from this day forward, for better or worse, for richer or poorer, in sickness and in health, to love and to cherish, till death do us part. . . ."

Those words were easy to say among the candles, in the lovely church, surrounded by people who love me, but now . . . .

The realities of life—hard work, pain, aging, poverty, criticism, failure, the disappointments of each day—descend like a cloud over the dream.

Will I keep my promise?

"His wife said to him, 'Are you still holding on to your integrity? Curse God and die.' He replied, 'You are talking like a foolish woman. Shall we accept good from God, and not trouble?' " (Job 2:9–10).

JOB

Why didn't he
  "curse God and die"
    as his wife advised?
What kept him sane
  when he had lost
      everything?
How did Job manage
  to maintain his integrity?

I probably would have given
      up
    given up on my friends
    given up on my faith
    given up on life.

Instead, Job accepted what
      God had allowed.
  "The Lord gives
    and the Lord takes away.
  Blessed be the name of the
      Lord."

Or, as Paul said,
  "I have learned
    in whatever state I am
      to be content."

Thanks, Lord, for Job's example.
  I can't say I want his problems
    but they sure do make mine
      look a lot smaller.

Jesus said, "In this world you will have trouble," but I find it hard to accept that it means me, too.

I see the suffering all around and feel sad, but when it happens to me, I'm tempted to think God isn't fair—or that He is punishing me for something.

It seems like Jesus should have promised us happiness instead of hardship, even though He Himself had more hardship than happiness. However, He did promise to give us joy—joy that runs deep and strong underneath the turbulence of life.

Can I trust God to use my difficult experiences to make a better person out of me?

"Although [Jesus] was a son, he learned obedience from what he suffered and, once made perfect, he became the source of eternal salvation for all who obey him" (Hebrews 5:8–9).

59

MARRIAGE TO A HARLOT WHO TURNED TO GOD

SALMON AND RAHAB

Joshua had sent two spies to the region of Jericho. They stopped for lodging at the house of Rahab, a harlot, who hid them under bales of flax on the rooftop and lied to their pursuers.

She told the spies that her people had heard about the mighty acts of their God in heaven who dried up the Red Sea and defeated enemies before them. She anticipated the defeat of Jericho and asked that her kindness to them be repaid by a promise to save her whole family when Jericho fell.

They made a solemn promise to honor her request, so she let them down by a rope to the outside of the city wall to escape their pursuers.

They asked her to hang a scarlet rope from that window and gather her family there so that their lives would be spared when the attack came.

Joshua honored this promise and saved Rahab's family. Rahab herself remained in Israel, married a man named Salmon, and gave birth to Boaz, the great grandfather of David, from whose lineage Jesus was born.

Bible Background: Joshua 2:1–21, 6:22–25, Ruth 4:18–22, Matthew 1:1–6.

SALMON

I just can't imagine
  marrying the city
    prostitute!
But that's what Salmon did!

Salmon—was he the
    adventurous spy
who entered Jericho
  and escaped
    because of Rahab's help?
Or was he a humble
    herdsmen
who didn't know or care
  about Rahab's reputation?

No matter who he was
  —spy or spectator,
    chief or shepherd—
he put the past behind him
  and helped her to do the
    same.

They had a son whose name
    was Boaz
  —remember him?—
a strong and upright man
    in Bethlehem
the father of Obed
  who was the father of
    Jesse
    the father of King
    David
    the forefather of Jesus
    Christ.

God, You had a reason for Rahab,
    didn't You?
and a reason for her being in
    Your family tree—
  the tree that became a cross?

Forgiveness is the most wonderful thing God could have thought up, because no person can undo one deed, unsay one word from the past. Every sin, every grievance, every intentioned hurt is real and wrong. The seriousness of it cannot be excused or explained away.

Only forgiveness can heal the past. In the alchemy of divine mercy the contamination is burned away, and we are clean and fit for God's good purpose.

What grievance do you need to forgive in order to be forgiven?

"Though your sins are like scarlet, they shall be as white as snow" (Isaiah 1:18b).

62

RAHAB

JUST AS SHE WAS . . .

Carmen cut my hair today
and we talked—
   actually, she talked and I
     listened
   and then I invited her to
     church.
She didn't say yes or no.
   Probably she's ashamed
     and embarrassed
    —feels as though
      everyone knows
      what's happened in her
      life.

I wanted to tell her about
     Rahab—
   Rahab, the town prostitute
   well-known at the inn
   well-liked by the men
  but one day her life
     changed
   and somehow she was
     convinced
     that the God of Israel
     accepted her
      just as she was.

How glad I am that Salmon accepted
     her too
   loved her enough to claim her as his
     own
   and marry her
     for better or for worse.

Acceptance is the clean bedrock foundation on which God builds a temple for His dwelling place. He clears away the rubble of past sins and failures and buries it all under the sea of forgetfulness. He remembers it against us no more and comes to live in our hearts.

Acceptance is not neutral indifference to the wrong we have done. It is not pretending that everything is OK. It is affirming the humanity and the value of another person in spite of his or her sin.

Acceptance is the Land of Beginning Again. Are you practicing acceptance in your marriage?

"Some of you were [sexually immoral]. But you were washed, you were sanctified, you were justified in the name of the Lord Jesus Christ and by the Spirit of our God" (1 Corinthians 6:11).

A JEWISH LEADER—
AND HER HUSBAND

DEBORAH AND LAPIDOTH

Deborah and Lapidoth were an unusual couple.

In this period of Israel's history the nation had no leadership. Former leaders like Joshua, who trusted the Lord, were dead. Every person did what was "right in his own eyes."

Soon, however, like little children, the children of Israel needed an arbitrator. And so Deborah, a mother in Israel, became a mother *to* Israel. She settled hot disputes in the cooling shade of her backyard palm tree. Perhaps husband Lapidoth played games with the children, teaching a second generation how to win and lose graciously, while their parents argued.

But God did not allow Deborah to stay in the shade; he called her into the heat of the battlefront. He spoke through her to appoint, encourage and accompany a hesitant hero, Barak, against the forces of King Jabin, a Canaanite king whose 900 iron chariots terrorized Israel. The battle was won, and this woman is remembered not only as a prophetess, but also as one of the great leaders of Israel.

And it seems to us that Deborah's husband, Lapidoth, must have been a great man as well—a man who was secure enough to be an enabler.

Bible Background: Judges 4:1–16, 5:1–15.

65

DEBORAH

MOTHER IN ISRAEL

What a woman
she must have been—
  out there on the
    battlefield
  with all the men
sitting at the conference
  table
   helping decide public
     policy
    instead of staying
     home
    and baking bread.

Deborah, called a mother in
  Israel!
Maybe that means she
  learned
 leadership and
   servanthood
discernment and patience
wisdom and hospitality
  through training her
  children
and then put those gifts to
  use
 with her people.

Sometimes it's hard to believe that God is training you for some future service while you are faithful in small things, behind the scenes, with your hands in the kitchen sink or wiping the noses of children.

It's hard to believe that people in the public eye will be more effective there if they have first learned to serve at home.

Public ministry and service, or a career, look so glamorous . . . but is there really any more important role in life than helping to guide the lives of little human beings into the goodness of God's will?

Are you encouraging each other to be faithful in family responsibilities?

"Instead, whoever wants to become great among you must first be your servant, and whoever wants to be first must be your slave—just as the Son of Man did not come to be served, but to serve, and to give his life as a ransom for many" (Matthew 20:26b–28).

LAPIDOTH

AN ENABLER

With a name like
Lapidoth,
   what chance did you have
    to make the headlines?
Especially when your wife
   was out confronting iron
      chariots
   with the leaders of Israel!
But Deborah could be trusted.
All Israel came to her for
      advice—
   a mother in Israel
    who held court under a
      palm tree.
And good ol' Lapidoth
   must have been an
      enabler—
   a man who was not less
    of a man
     because his wife was a
     great woman.

Some couples compete rather than cooperate.

When a man is secure enough to live confidently and gratefully with a gifted and prominent wife, he gains—rather than loses—stature in the eyes of others. Her wisdom multiplies his own; his eyes and ears are opened to see and hear truths revealed to both of them in the fuller dimensions of both the male and female perspectives of God.

Thus do two become one, not only in mind and heart, but also in purpose and accomplishment.

Are you and your spouse working as true teammates in your home and in God's service?

"Submit to one another out of reverence for Christ" (Ephesians 5:21).

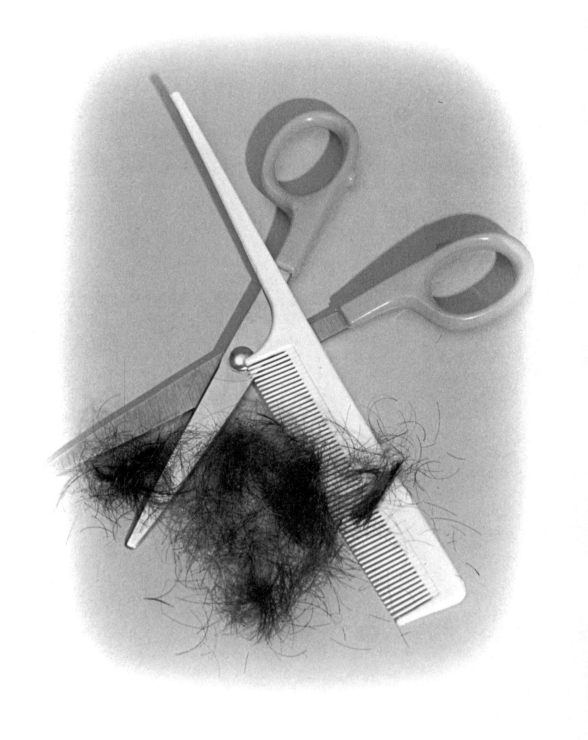

STRENGTH AND WEAKNESS

SAMSON AND DELILAH

Samson's birth was announced by a messenger from God who also gave specific instructions for Samson's prenatal and postnatal care. His humble parents eagerly obeyed every detail.

When Samson grew up, he was blessed and inspired by the Spirit of the Lord.

Samson insisted, however, on marrying a Philistine woman. At their wedding feast he proposed a riddle to his 30 groomsmen, offering a sizeable bet that they could not solve it. His wife begged him to tell her the answer—and then she told the men. Great turmoil followed, and eventually his wife and her father were killed.

Samson was strong and wily enough to kill a lion with his bare hands, to kill a thousand men with a mere jawbone, to catch 300 foxes, to carry the posts and gates of a city to the top of a hill. But he was weak and naive in the presence of evil women.

After judging and defending Israel for 20 years, Samson was enticed and deceived by the Philistine woman Delilah. She tricked him into telling her the secret of his strength, but even after she had his hair cut, he did not realize that the Lord had departed from him.

The plot to weaken and capture Samson succeeded. His enemies, the Philistines, gouged out his eyes and forced him to grind grain in the prison house.

Over a period of time Samson's hair grew again. At a great celebration for their god Dagon, the Philistines called their captive to entertain them.

"O Sovereign Lord, remember me. . . . please strengthen me just once more," Samson prayed. He grasped the central supporting pillars of the huge building, pulling it down on the crowd of 3,000 spectators. More enemies were killed at his death than in all his life.

Bible Background: Judges 13–16, Hebrews 11:32.

SAMSON

If it feels good, do it!
  they said.
I did it—*my* way.

I went against everything
  I had been taught
and I did it—*my* way.

I gave in to the lust of the
        flesh
  and lost my strength.
I followed the lust of the eyes
  and lost my sight.
I desired the pride of life
  and lost my life.

It didn't feel good
    in the end
  when I did it
    my way.

What could God have done
        with my life
  if I had lived it *His* way?

There seems to be a "little god" sitting on a wobbly throne inside every human heart, a cocky little god who says, "But . . . I know best." He echoes the doubt the serpent planted in the mind of the first woman in the Garden of Eden: "Did God say . . . ?"

And then he gives his own interpretation of the rules for life.

Before we realize how far away from God's truth and will we are, Satan may have led us so far down some path of self-will or self-indulgence that, like Samson, we do not even realize we are lost!

At first we *would* not do God's will. Later, perhaps, we *could* not.

Will you check your spiritual compass to make sure you are on course?

"There is a way that seems right to a man, but in the end it leads to death" (Proverbs 14:12 and 16:25).

DELILAH

STRENGTH AND SEDUCTION

I can conquer him, she
said—
  the strongest man on earth.
I can conquer him
  because my will
    is stronger than his.

He talks of vows to his God
  but he's already broken one
    —his vow of purity—
      why not another?

I know what he wants.
  More important, I know
      what *I* want.
I'll steal his secret
  when he's most vulnerable
    and then I'll ask, so
      innocently:
  But how can it be wrong
    when it feels so right?

Our human need for affirmation, for recognition, for respect, for feeling important to someone, is often unfulfilled.

We are so quick to criticize, so slow to commend, often because we ourselves feel so insecure.

The people of God often fail—in their friendships, in their fellowships and in their families—to obey the scriptural admonition to edify, to build up one another.

Then Satan introduces a willing conspirator who seduces people, young and old, first into activities of doubtful value, then into the self-deceptions of drinking or drugs or illicit sex. False pleasure centers in the brain and soul are stimulated, and we are sucked deeper and deeper into the vortex of moral failure and despair.

Can you identify any subtle seducer in your life?

_____

"With persuasive words she led him astray; she seduced him with her smooth talk. All at once he followed her like an ox going to the slaughter, like a deer stepping into a noose" (Proverbs 7:21–22).

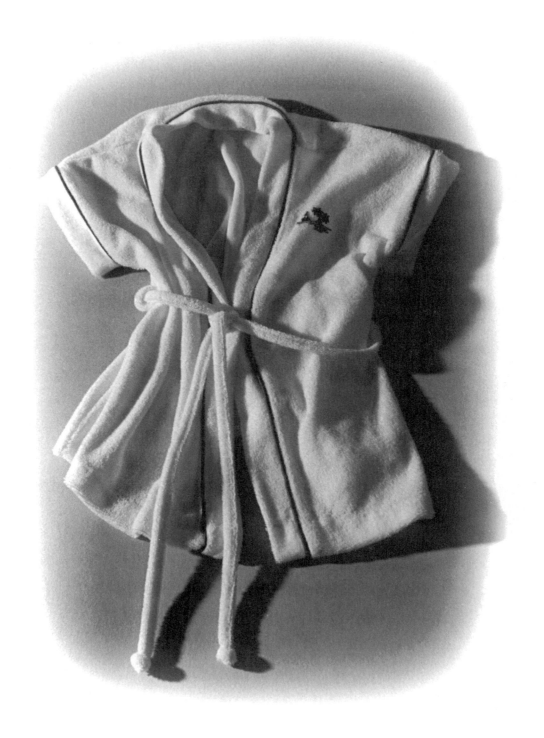

DISAPPOINTMENT OF BARRENNESS

HANNAH AND ELKANAH

Elkanah was a devout and just husband who faithfully worshiped God and carefully allotted sacrificial offerings for his children and his two wives.

At every yearly sacrifice Peninnah, the wife with children, would taunt Hannah, who had no children and suffered public disgrace because of it. Hannah's grief was so great that she could not eat.

Elkanah, who loved her in spite of her childlessness, tried to comfort her by reminding her of his love for her. But she cried and prayed in the agony of her heart until the old priest Eli said her prayer would be answered.

It was! She gave birth to a son and refrained from attending the yearly sacrifices until Samuel was weaned. This she did because she had resolved in her heart to honor God by presenting her baby Samuel himself to the service of God for as long as he lived.

What a grand worship service it was when Hannah gave her son to the service of God. She filled the air with her songs of praise, even though she would now be able to see her son only once a year when she brought him a new coat to cover his body.

How hard it must have been to entrust him into Eli's care, when Eli's own sons had gone astray. She must also have covered him with prayer!

Bible Background: 1 Samuel 1:1–28, 2:1–12.

73

ELKANAH

CAUGHT IN THE MIDDLE

I sure wouldn't want to be
in Elkanah's shoes.

I have enough trouble
      understanding *one*
      woman
    —and I hate it when she
      cries!—
      and this guy Elkanah
      had one wife who cried a
      lot
and the other wife
      probably yelled a lot
    and there he was
    caught in the middle.

He loved the one who cried a
      lot
    —out of her need for
      children—
and it doesn't seem like he
      loved the other one
    who had his children.

I guess that's why
  You made one woman
    for one man.

God ordained marriage to demonstrate Christ's unconditional, never-ending love and faithfulness.

But, being human, we need a lifetime of practice with one man, one woman. God said, "Two shall become one!" He never said, "Three or four. . . ."

Giving up on one marriage and starting over on another one is not progress toward Christian maturity. It is going back to the starting line every time.

Every marriage has difficulties, because there are no really compatible people. We have to learn to walk together, adjusting our pace to each other and to daily agendas.

Will you do that faithfully until death?

". . . husbands ought to love their wives as their own bodies. He who loves his wife loves himself. After all, no one ever hated his own body, but he feeds and cares for it, just as Christ does the church—for we are members of his body. 'For this reason a man will leave his father and mother and be united to his wife, and the two will become one flesh' " (Ephesians 5:28–31).

74

HANNAH

What are the reasons
I want a child, Lord?
  a feeling of usefulness?
      fulfillment?
  an extension of myself?

Would I be willing to
  give back a child to You
    if I were given one?
  hand him over
    to an old priest
      who had already failed
        with two sons of his
          own?

Hannah did.
  She asked for a man-child
    who would lead the
        nation Israel
      back to God.

To do that
  she had to give her boy-
        child
    to God—to use
      in whatever way He
        chose.

Our children are the earth's most precious resource. They are the very fruit of our bodies and of our being, our "one flesh" creations. The nerve and sinew of both father and mother are enmeshed and entwined eternally in them, an unbreakable bond. What awesome responsibility we feel!

As with all other trusts committed by God to our temporal care, however, we are only stewards. These children are His, and they will be ours forever—treasures in heaven—when we give them to God and let His purposes for them guide our brief guidance of them.

Are you bringing your children daily to God in humble prayer?

"O Lord Almighty, if you will only look upon your servant's misery and remember me, and not forget your servant but give her a son, then I will give him to the Lord for all the days of his life" (1 Samuel 1:11).

WHAT'S IN A NAME

NAOMI AND ELIMELECH

His name, Elimelech, meant "God is my King." Her name, Naomi, meant "pleasant." They looked forward to rewarding days of serving Jehovah in peace and prosperity.

But since they named their sons Mahlon and Chilion, meaning "sickly" and "pining," we can assume that life brought adversity. Bethlehem, the "house of bread," began to suffer days of famine.

And so the family moved to Moab, "land of the proud," peopled by the descendants of Lot. Mahlon and Chilion married Moabite girls, but died young and childless. Elimelech died also, and Naomi was left alone, in a strange land.

Is it any wonder she wanted to change her name?

The story, however, is not over. Although God's own people would not trust Him, He worked through a Moabitess who made a choice when she said to her mother-in-law: "Your people will be my people and your God my God."

Bible Background: Ruth 1–4.

77

ELIMELECH

FOOD THAT ENDURES

Why did Elimelech
decide
  to move to Moab—
    "land of the proud"
    descendants of Lot and
      his daughter
    rebels against the one
      true God?
But then
  wasn't he just trying to
      provide
    food for his family
    a better way of life
      than they could find
        in famine-stricken
        Bethlehem
          (ironically, the
          "house of bread")?

In his attempt to provide
  for his sickly sons
    Elimelech lost them.
    They died.
    He died.
Did they die spiritually first?

It's difficult—and risky—to live in the world and not allow the world to live in us.

When a family is hungry or cold or needy in any way, our natural instinct is to care for the body first, to move to a better job and higher pay, often without counting the eternal cost, without responding to the hunger for righteousness.

It's hard to decide when enough is enough, to be satisfied with a simple but sufficient lifestyle.

Will your children live or die spiritually as a result of plans you are now making?

"Do not work for food that spoils, but for food that endures to eternal life, which the Son of Man will give you" (John 6:27).

NAOMI

MARA DAYS

Call me no more Naomi,"
the once-pleasant woman
said.
"Just call me Mara.
The El Shaddai's dealt
bitterly with me."

And there are times
when I feel also
"Naomi days" are far
behind
and "Mara days"
are all that lie ahead.

And yet
it is in times like these
El Shaddai shows me
the meaning of His
name—
the power and
strength of El
the tender Shaddai
love
power coupled with
compassion
might with great
tenderness
strength with unfailing
love.

The old promises echo and reecho in our marriages—"for richer or poorer, for better or worse. . . ." When the dark side of those promises rears its ugly head, we often falter. We sometimes blame God, as Naomi did.

Her husband and sons were dead and buried in a foreign land. Life seemed futile, a series of one bitter day—"Mara day"—hopelessly yearning into another.

Then God brought a new light into her life, when one son's wife made her a glowing promise: "Where you go, I will go. . . ."

The name *Shaddai* is derived from the Hebrew word *shad*, meaning the breast of the nursing mother.

What does that tell you about God's parent nature?

"No eye has seen, no ear has heard, no mind has conceived what God has prepared for those who love him" (1 Corinthians 2:9).

A WIDOW FINDS
AN HONORABLE
HUSBAND

RUTH AND BOAZ

Ruth was Naomi's widowed daughter-in-law, who accompanied Naomi back to her home country. There she met the wealthy and generous Boaz, kinsman of Naomi, while gleaning grain from his fields.

He praised Ruth's devotion to the highly respected Naomi and invited her to have lunch with him and his reapers.

Naomi then instructed Ruth in the courtship customs of her country, which required next of kin to marry a widow. Ruth found Boaz asleep on the threshing floor and lay down at his feet. When he awoke he was startled to find her there. She reminded him of his responsibility to a relative's widow.

Boaz followed custom carefully by checking first with a nearer and younger relative, who had the first option to marry Ruth. Since the other man declined to marry her, Boaz called a council of elders, in whose presence he was granted rights to purchase Naomi's land and take Ruth, the Moabitess, as his wife.

That is how this foreign woman became the great grandmother of King David, ancestor of Jesus.

Bible Background: Ruth 1–4.

RUTH

FACTS, NOT FAULTS

If anything happened to my
mother
    I'd want to be right there
      to take care of her
      to do whatever I could.
But if it were my
      mother-in-law
    would I react the same?
This is what Ruth said to her
      mother-in-law:
    "Don't make me leave you.
    I want to go wherever
      you go,
      and to live wherever
      you live;
    your people shall be my
      people
      and your God shall be
      my God;
    I want to die where you
      die,
      and be buried there.
    May the Lord do terrible
      things to me
      if I allow anything but
      death
      to separate us."
Lord, I don't have that kind
    of love.
    I don't have Ruth's kind of
      servant spirit.
There are some things about
    his family
    I just don't like—

things that irritate me
    different ways of doing things
    different ways of thinking
    different lifestyles
      from what I'm accustomed to.
And . . . I guess he feels the same way
    about my family—
    he probably thinks we're weird
      sometimes.
I never realized that before.

Differences are just facts. They are not faults. You are simply different from me in many ways—not defective.

When we make unkind or condescending remarks about the other sex, the other generation, the other culture, we disparage the wisdom of God in Christ in whom there is no sexual, racial, age or cultural bias. Christ came to break down the walls between people.

When we respect and embrace the differentness of other people, we can become truly *one.*

Do you feel that *oneness* in your relationship?

"We who are strong ought to bear with the failings of the weak and not to please ourselves. Each of us should please his neighbor for his good, to build him up" (Romans 15:1–2).

BOAZ

IN-LAWS

Holidays can become a
problem, Lord.
  Giving both families equal
      time
can be difficult
    especially when one is far
      away.
Sometimes I feel like just
      staying home,
    ignoring both families,
but that brings
      repercussions
and she'd cry the day
      away,
    I'm sure.
Seems lately it's become a
      contest
  whose family comes first
  whose family gets more
      gifts
        bigger gifts
        better gifts.
On holidays, Lord, I get so
      tired
  of talking to great-aunts
    and smiling ("What a
      nice young man!")
  when I really want to
      watch the game
    which is what my
      brothers would be
      doing
    at *my* home!

But today's man of the hour
    —his name means "strength"—
  must have welcomed his wife's (get
      this!)
  former mother-in-law
    into his home—
    she became his son's nanny.
His name was Boaz
  and he married Ruth.
    Her name means "friendship."
That sure was a test
  of strength *and* friendship.

Who am I?" cry people who are
having an "identity crisis."

    Identity is not static. It is not something about yourself that you find and keep forever. I am not now who I was. I am, hopefully, being shaped into the image of Christ.

    Jesus knew who He was, where He came from and where He was going, so He knew *who to be* to *whoever was there*, in His presence, without defensiveness or partiality. Personhood emerges in relationships.

    The Son of God could stoop down and wash feet without any damage to His self-esteem. Are you that secure?

"Serve one another in love" (Galatians 5:13b).

WISDOM AND FOOLISHNESS
ABIGAIL AND NABAL

For some reason unknown to us, the beautiful, intelligent and gracious Abigail was given in marriage to the wealthy Nabal, who was surly and mean and called The Fool.

Near Nabal's property David and his soldiers were hiding out to avoid encounters with the soldiers of King Saul. King Saul was out to kill the young hero who was already appointed as the next king of Israel.

David's band protected the properties in the area and depended upon the land owners for food and supplies. When Nabal was asked for food, he angrily refused. So David ordered 400 soldiers to destroy Nabal's men.

When the servants told Abigail what was happening, she quickly gathered a large donation of supplies, went out to meet David and his band, and begged his forgiveness for her husband's insults. Then she reminded David not to soil his conscience with bloodshed and pled for protection. David agreed.

When she told her husband, who was recovering from a night of drunkenness, what she had done, he had a heart attack and died 10 days later.

David himself then married this remarkable woman.

Bible Background: 1 Samuel 25:1–42.

85

ABIGAIL

DISAPPOINTMENT

I think of Abigail
and of what she went
through
with Nabal, her husband.

He was a drunken oaf
a big bully
the kind of man
no woman should have
to live with
—but many do.

The women who love too
much
the women who have
nowhere to go
the women who think
they're not worth
helping—
weeping
lonely
unhelped women.

Is there an abused woman in
my neighborhood?
How can I help her to
believe in You
—and in herself—
a woman made in the
image of God?

Unlike Abigail, today's woman chooses the man she marries.

Even so, sometimes marriage seems too hard, too long. Sometimes marriage commitments cause you to wish for a shorter life. This is especially true if you have chosen a spouse who disappoints you and hurts you in many ways.

Of course, life in general presents many disappointments, losses, hardships. When circumstances do not change, when it's very difficult to live with your own personal choices, with the promises you have made, you must make every effort to seek counsel and support from true friends who can help your marriage heal its wounds or help you survive the difficulties.

Trust God to help you keep your promises and do your part of His will.

Do you have a support group to help you do this?

_____

"His name was Nabal and his wife, a beautiful and very intelligent woman, was named Abigail. But the man, who was a descendant of Caleb, was uncouth, churlish, stubborn, and ill-mannered" (1 Samuel 25:30 LB).

86

NABAL

ANGER

When I think about the
Nabals I have known
  maybe even grown up with
    I get angry.

The know-it-all Nabals
  the men who always get
    their own way
    who always do their
     own thing
    who ignore everyone
     else's best interests
  —selfish, self-centered,
    childish Nabals.
Yes, I get angry! Any real
    man would.
But my anger must be
    expressed in
     constructive ways
  or it will accomplish
    nothing.

A real man rescues a
     battered woman
    comforts an abused
     child
    gets help for an
     alcoholic father.
The right kind of anger
    confronts a bad
     situation
  instead of walking away.

And my anger can insure
  —because I've seen the results of *his*
    kind of anger—
  that I will never become a Nabal
    myself.

Some men try to "prove their man-hood" by muscle, mouth or manipulation. They use power. Some men ignore or "use" women in their lives—their mothers, their wives, their daughters—in selfish or evil ways.

Such men never learn how to be helpful or protective of other persons. They never experience the wonderful and joyful strength of gentleness.

Such men never learn that giving is the most successful way of exercising strength and power; for it is in such giving that they, themselves, receive the most in return.

What behaviors help you to feel good about yourself?

"One man gives freely, yet gains even more; another withholds unduly, but comes to poverty. A generous man will prosper; he who refreshes others will himself be refreshed" (Proverbs 11:24–25).

A TERRIBLE SIN

DAVID AND BATHSHEBA

King David's army was at war, but David was relaxing in his palace. While walking on the roof he saw the lovely Bathsheba bathing below and sent his men to bring her to him to spend the night.

Later, when she sent word that she was pregnant, David quickly arranged a visit home from the army for Bathsheba's husband, Uriah.

This loyal young soldier, instead of going home, spent the night on the palace steps with the servants. He explained that he could not accept special privileges with his wife when his fellow soldiers and the ark of the covenant—the symbol of God's presence—were out in the fields.

Having failed in this attempt to cover up Bathsheba's pregnancy, David ordered his commander Joab to put Uriah in the front line of battle, where he was indeed killed.

Bathsheba mourned the death of her brave young husband. After the her period of mourning was over, David ordered her to be brought to his house as a wife, and she gave birth to David's son.

But what David had done displeased the Lord. The prophet Nathan pronounced God's punishment on David, including the death of Bathsheba's child. David confessed and repented. His anguish and misery before his repentance are vividly described in the Psalms.

Bible Background: 2 Samuel 11:1–27, 12:1–24, Psalms 32, 51.

89

DAVID

WANDERING

I can just imagine David
 caged, catlike, bored
 pacing the rooftop
  restlessly
 wishing he had gone to
  war.
Then he turns
 and looks over the city
  one more time
 and sees her.

Suddenly, life becomes a
  challenge
 once again
a new possibility for
  conquest.

"She is Bathsheba . . . wife of
  Uriah."
The messenger's words
 do not decrease
  his conquer-lust.

Lust led to deceit
 and then to murder
 and later rape
  more death
  and mutiny
all because one king
 was wandering across a
  rooftop
 when he should have
  been at war
 against the enemy.

Beware of every subtle temptation or contrivance to experience a relationship with someone other than your spouse.

It starts with little mental meanderings, little "legitimate diversions" from the responsibilities of loving your own spouse—when disappointment, frustration or boredom with routine hits you.

Marriage is not a daily appointment with glamor and excitement; even kings and presidents have dirty underwear. Marriage is laying down your life in loving sacrifice.

Are you winning on the battleground of your temptations?

———————————

"Each one is tempted when, by his own evil desire, he is dragged away and enticed. Then, after desire has conceived, it gives birth to sin; and sin, when it is full-grown, gives birth to death" (James 1:14–15).

90

BATHSHEBA

CHOICES

Seems like Bathsheba had
very little choice
  in the matter, Lord.
I mean, when the king called,
    you went!
Certainly a night in bed
  with a handsome king
    was preferable to
      "off with her head!"
But did she feel she had a
      choice?

Sometimes, Lord, I feel caged
      in too
  in no-win situations
    and saying NO point-
      blank
      doesn't even seem
        like an option.
Black and white merges into
      gray
  and I lose all perspective
    on what is right.

Is it because I make myself
      vulnerable
  by bathing in the open
    too often?

How much responsibility should a woman take to avoid becoming an object of "the lust of the eyes" of men?

Men are more likely to be turned on by what they see, while women respond more readily to feeling loved and cared for.

Wordly display of possessions or physical beauty has caused much envy and craving and self-depreciation by the have-nots. Comparison often leads to covetousness, to breaking the 10th commandment. The media, movies and magazines contrive to lead us astray.

It is so tempting to conform to the worldly fashions of near-nudity. How much of your body do you reserve for no other admiring eyes than those of your husband?

"I also want women to dress modestly, with decency and propriety . . . with good deeds, appropriate for women who profess to worship God" (1 Timothy 2:9–10).

AVAILABILITY TO GOD

ESTHER AND XERXES

Hitler hated the Jews—we all know that—but do you remember Haman, who also tried to wipe out God's chosen people? His plan was foiled, however, by a lovely young woman who "just happened" to be in the right place at the right time.

The place was Persia, the city of Susa. The Jewish nation, because of its disobedience to God, had been taken captive by the Babylonians, who in turn had been conquered by the Persians. The time was between 486 and 465 B.C., when Xerxes was king of Persia.

The lovely young woman was Esther, who had been raised by her cousin Mordecai. Mordecai was instrumental in bringing Esther, without revealing her Jewish identity, to the attention of the king, who was looking for a new queen. Thus Esther risked her own life in order to save her people.

Was it coincidental that Esther found herself chosen to replace Xerxes's former queen at just the right time, when her people were desperately in need of someone with access to the king? Because of her willingness to intercede, risking her life in the process, Esther became God's means of saving the Jewish nation.

Bible Background: Esther 1–10.

93

ESTHER

She lived in a time
  when a woman's life was
     not her own.

She was a woman sent to the
      throne
  "for such a time as this"
    —not because God
        invented beauty
        contests
    —not because God
        wanted her to marry
        a pagan king
    —not because God
        approved of harems
but because
  God had a unique time
      and place for Esther
      just as He does for me.

Perhaps you know a Christian woman who chose to marry a man who was not a believer. He made glowing promises of support and noninterference with her church life.

Instead, he keeps her in a torture chamber of indifference or coldly calculated criticism or outspoken rejection. Or perhaps he simply keeps her on display, hoping her faith will be his good-luck charm.

There is no fellowship, unless in bed or at breakfast. There is no genuine *oneness*. Both husband and wife may suffer unspoken pain, the pain of living a divided life.

Will she compromise or complain away her peace of mind? Or will he become a believer because of the beauty of her holiness and the strength of her faith?

Perhaps . . . perhaps not.

"Wives, . . . be submissive to your husbands, so that, if any of them do not believe the word, they may be won over without words by the behavior of their wives, when they see the purity and reverence of your lives" (1 Peter 3:1–2).

XERXES

"I WANTED TO . . ."

Today, at noon, we met for lunch
  and you were late
  —you're never late—
  and I began to worry.

Me, worry?
  I would have laughed a
      year ago
    at the thought
  but I could not deny the
      fact
    that fear was closing in.
    The roads were icy,
      the traffic heavy.
  You hate driving in bad
      weather.

Then you walked in
  and time stood still.
You never looked more
      beautiful
  cheeks reddened by the
      cold
  eyes shining
    sparkling
    searching for me.

I wanted to jump up from
    the table
    take you in my arms
    tell you I loved you
      more than life itself

confess how scared I'd been
  of losing you.

Instead, I looked at my watch
  and fiddled with the menu
    as you apologized.
  "Where've you been?" I said quite
    calmly.
  "I'll be late getting back to work."

Perhaps you know a Christian woman who chose to marry a believer—and yet she, too, is kept in the torture chamber of indifference. King Xerxes neglected to call Esther to come to him for 30 days at a time. Some husbands simply fail to express their appreciation and love.

Taking-for-granted is such a common sin that we scarcely know we are sinning. We may be accustomed to resisting evil, but we often fail to do good things. We commit over and over again some sin of omission.

What perverse pride and insecurity keep us from letting our beloveds hear how dear they are to us?

Will you hug them and tell them now?

"Anyone, then, who knows the good he ought to do and doesn't do it, sins" (James 4:17).

MARRIED TO AN ADULTERESS
HOSEA AND GOMER

In the case of Hosea, the prophet, God not only gave him a message to speak, He made his *life* a message.

God told Hosea to marry an adulterous woman and have children by her to show how much God loved His people.

After the birth of three children she left him again, and the Lord commanded Hosea to show his love again. This time Hosea bought her off an auction block for prostitutes.

Then he told her, "You are to live with me many days; you must not be a prostitute or be intimate with any man, and I will live with you."

God said of His people, "I will punish her for the days she . . . went after her lovers, but me she forgot. . . . [But] I am now going to allure her; I will lead her into the desert and speak tenderly to her. There I will give her back her vineyards, and will make the Valley of Achor a door of hope. There she will sing as in the days of her youth. . . ."

Bible Background: Hosea 1:2–8, 2:13–16, 3:1–3.

97

HOSEA

SUCH LOVE

This guy Hosea is unreal,
Lord—
    the way he kept right on
       loving his wife
    no matter what she did.
    And she was a real hellion!

He even bought her off the
      auction block
    after she had sold herself
      to other men!

Surely You don't expect that
      kind of love
    from me, Lord!

Lord?

I mean, she didn't deserve it!

Lord???

Divorce is a contradiction of God's never-ending love and inexhaustible reservoir of forgiveness.

God hates divorce because it spells unforgiveness, rejection, abandonment. God will never leave you nor forsake you.

Divorce carries the banner of rights and abdicates the seat of responsibility.

While we were yet sinners, Christ died for us. God used Hosea to demonstrate to his wife, Gomer, His own unconditional love.

Will you really be faithful in loving your spouse, for better or worse, until death?

"Guard yourself in your spirit, and do not break faith with the wife of your youth. 'I hate divorce,' says the Lord God of Israel, 'and I hate a man's covering himself with violence, . . . ' says the Lord Almighty" (Malachi 2:15b–16).

GOMER

REDEEMED

I imagine Gomer felt
  that no one
    could ever love her again
      want her
      even look at her.
Now everyone knew the
      truth about her.

There have been times, Lord
  when I was sure
    if you knew how I really
      felt
      what I was really
        thinking
      what I had really done
You wouldn't love me any
      more
      want me
      even look at me.

And then I told You . . .
  and You said,
    "I forgive you, my child.
      I'll always love you."

Christ does not find the church pure and lovely. His love *makes* her pure and lovely if she submits to Him.

Jesus is never surprised or dismayed by our ugliness. He knows us as well as He knew His disciples: traitors, deniers, schemers—frightened, faithless men. He changed 11 of them into loyal lovers.

Does your spouse disappoint you? Christ's love, working through you, can cleanse and wash away the stains of faults and failures, and you will have a new wife, a new husband.

Are you like Hosea? or Gomer? or both?

Can you forgive like Jesus?

"Husbands, love your wives, just as Christ loved the church and gave himself up for her to make her holy, cleansing her by the washing with water through the word, and to present her to himself as a radiant church, without stain or wrinkle or any other blemish, but holy and blameless" (Ephesians 5:25–27).

A DELAYED ANSWER TO PRAYER

ELIZABETH AND ZACHARIAS

They were both old; they were both righteous; they were both blameless in the sight of the Lord. They had hoped for a child for years, but when an angel appeared to the old man as he went about his priestly duties in the temple, he couldn't believe the good news. Now, in their old age, they were to have a son!

As a sign that the angel's words were indeed true, Zacharias lost his ability to spread the good news. He lost his voice for nine months. But I imagine he lost no time in writing a note to his elderly wife, who probably squinted over his confused scrawl in bewilderment.

And then she rejoiced: "The Lord has done this for me. . . . In these days he has shown his favor and taken away my disgrace among the people."

Six months before the birth of Jesus, John the Baptist was born. He was Jesus' cousin, and he would also be His forerunner.

Bible Background: Luke 1:5–25, 57–80.

101

ELIZABETH

MATURITY

It's so exciting, Lord, to see
You working
   in older people's lives—
      people who have grown
         in your love
         your joy
         your peace
   people like Elizabeth and
      Zacharias.

Oh, Lord, may I have that
      kind of faith
   when I get to that age—
      the wisdom
      the discernment
      the lack of jealousy
I see reflected in
      Elizabeth's greeting
   of her cousin Mary
      who was to bear a son
      who would be greater
         than Elizabeth's
      yearned-for son.

How I love her gentle, joyful
      servant spirit
   in her salutation of Mary:
      "Blessed are you among
         women
   and blessed is the child you
      will bear.
      But why am I so favored
   that the mother of my Lord
      should come to me?"

Growing old gracefully and behaving graciously is not a choice that can be made late in life.

Don't compete or criticize or be catty. Paul told Titus to tell the older women to train the younger women to love. The best way to do that is to love them yourself. You are already older than somebody.

Begin now to open your heart and reach out your hands. Cultivate a generous spirit that especially enhances the fellowship of femaleness—women understanding, loving one another at all stages of life.

Are you part of a fellowship of godly women?

———————

"Speak to one another with psalms, hymns and spiritual songs. Sing and make music in your heart to the Lord, always giving thanks to God the Father for everything, in the name of our Lord Jesus Christ" (Ephesians 5:19–20).

ZACHARIAS

TONGUE-TIED

Strange story—
  an old man struck dumb
    unable to speak
      for nine long months
    because he couldn't
        believe
    his old wife could
        conceive
      the son they both
        desired
        above all else.

Dear God,
  if I were struck dumb
    every time I doubted You
I'd be a man of few words!

And yet
  when his tongue was
      "loosed"
    his very first words
      were words of praise!
        Not "It's about time!"
        or "What's going on
          here?"
      but words of praise.

Lord, teach me to know
  when to close my mouth
    before You have to do it
      for me.

Sometimes the longing of a man for a son or a daughter or some other wonderful thing is expressed in prayers so loud and persistent that the still small voice of God cannot be heard, and the very answer that God gives goes unnoticed.

When longing or loneliness strain every nerve and drain away every last vestige of your faith, Stop! Look! Listen! And give thanks for all that you can now see. The footsteps of God are here, and He is surely working for you.

Will you hold each other and pray every day through the doubting times?

"As the heavens are higher than the earth, so are my ways higher than your ways and my thoughts than your thoughts" (Isaiah 55:9).

A MARRIAGE THAT DIDN'T HAVE A CHANCE

MARY AND JOSEPH

All the world loves a baby"—but not its unwed mother! The relationship of Mary and Joseph seemingly got off to a bad start, with the potential for divorce present before the marriage even began.

The bride-to-be was pregnant, and someone had to tell the prospective groom, since he was not the father.

Divorce was permissible during the engagement, if there was proof of unfaithfulness, so Joseph thought about divorcing Mary quietly, privately. But then he heard a voice, a voice which told him a highly improbable story—that God was the Father of the baby.

Joseph knew how to discern the voice of God from the voices of men. He faced the difficulties that lay ahead, married the pregnant Mary and refrained from exercising his conjugal rights until after Jesus was born.

No wonder Joseph was God's choice for His Son's earthly father!

Bible Background: Isaiah 7:10–14, Matthew 1:18–25, Luke 1:26–38.

105

MARY

She faced the loneliest of
lives,
   the worst disgrace
     a Hebrew girl could
      know.
She could be taken out
      beyond the gates
  and stoned
   ignored by friends and
     family,
    lost, alone—
all this because her heart was
    open
  to His voice.
Her words come gently,
  urging me
   toward choice:
"Behold, behold . . . the
    handmaid of the
    Lord."

"Behold . . . a sword
  shall pierce thy heart also!"
Strange promise of great
    favor thus bestowed:
a rainbow arched through
    gently falling rain
erasing memories of the
    lightning's pain
a promise of new covenant
    life again!
"Behold, behold . . . the hand-
    maid of the Lord."

If angels appeared more often on the threshold of our daily lives, it would be so much easier, we think, to say, "Yes, Lord"—yes to womanhood, to duty, to privilege and to pain.

It is often lonely and unheralded to choose to be wife, childbearer, mother, when many voices try to drown out the satisfactions of commitment to the noble career of nurturing human beings.

It may be even more difficult for some women to forego those possibilities in womanhood and say "Yes, Lord" to singleness or barrenness.

Can you trust God to bless and use you as you are?

" 'I am the Lord's servant,' Mary answered. 'May it be to me as you have said' " (Luke 1:38a).

JOSEPH

Legally, he could have had
her stoned.
   Instead, he stayed the hand
      of human justice.
He could have totally
      rejected her.
   Instead, he proved his
      respect for her.
He had every right to revile
      her.
   Instead, he revealed his
      love for her.

He waited an additional nine
      months
   for the consummation of
      their marriage
   when he could have
      demanded
      his rights as a husband.
He believed an angel in a
      dream
   when his life had turned
      into
   a nightmare.
He listened to God's voice
   instead of the voices of
      men.

Thank You, God, for giving me Joseph
   as a role model—
      an unassuming carpenter
      who was unafraid
         of what people would say.

Celibate love sounds like an impossibility in a day when "making love" is equated with sex. To deny normal sexual desire for the higher good of the one loved, to say no to self in order to say yes to a loved one's need of space or privacy or tender care is such a spectacle of sacrificial love that it rises to the nostrils of God as an aroma of His son Jesus.

All of us must learn to love celibately or we will never know how to love sexually in marriage.

Sex often short-circuits the energizing current of *agape* love. Sex should be the last movement in a symphony of love.

Have you found that to be so?

"And live a life of love, just as Christ loved us and gave himself up for us as a fragrant offering and sacrifice to God" (Ephesians 5:2).

SHE WANTED THE BEST FOR HER FAMILY

SALOME AND ZEBEDEE

Salome was an assertive woman with strong political interests, married to a fisherman whose consuming passion may have been the mending of nets.

The Bible tells us nothing about their relationship. Historians say that Zebedee's business was so successful that he marketed his fish in Jerusalem as well as in their home town of Bethsaida, near Capernaum. Perhaps Salome tasted just enough of city life to give her an appetite for political power—vicariously, of course, through her sons. No Jewish woman of that day could hope for a closer connection.

So Salome came to Jesus one day and asked that her sons be granted positions of power and authority in Jesus' coming kingdom. Unexpectedly, Jesus responded with questions that Salome probably did not understand: "Can you drink the cup I am going to drink? Can you be baptized with the baptism I am baptized with?"

Jesus' eyes searched Salome's soul as He said gently: "Whoever wants to be great among you must be your servant."

Did Salome go home to tell Zebedee her new understanding of greatness? Did Salome and Zebedee ever come to understand Jesus' kind of kingdom? We wonder.

We do know that Salome continued to follow Jesus, to care for His needs and surely those of her sons. On Good Friday, at Calvary, Salome was still watching and listening, continuing to learn the significance of Jesus' questions.

Bible Background: Matthew 20:20–28.

109

ZEBEDEE

SONS OF THUNDER

Were James and John
called
    "sons of thunder"
        because ol' Zebedee
            shook the heavens
                with his anger?

Was one son like him—
    "like father, like son"?
        Was that James?

And did another
    shrink from the thunder
    hide from the lightning
    avoid the storms
    and bask in the Son-love
        of a heavenly Father?
            Was that John?

It's easy to see how all of our parents failed to behave in wise and responsible ways. It's easy to blame them for our own lack of wisdom or responsiveness to our family members.

We say, "I am this way because my mother did . . . my dad did—or never did—certain things."

Some of us have never "put away childish things." We make excuses for ourselves and hide behind the failures of parents, teachers, leaders of the past.

That is much easier to do than to make the mature choice to be the man, the woman, that God wants us to be, here and now.

What kind of person are you choosing to be?

———————

"How great is the love the Father has lavished on us, that we should be called children of God!" (1 John 3:1a).

SALOME

PASSIVITY AND POWER

What was it like
to be the wife
of the father
of the sons of thunder?

I imagine
you had to be rather
assertive
to be heard
above the thunder!

Salome was.
She asked for positions of
power
for her sons
in a future kingdom.
She didn't realize
she was really asking
for box seats
viewing a cross.

People often inherit strong personality traits. Sometimes they develop them in order to survive a difficult childhood.

Sometimes a woman becomes assertive or dominant in a family because the man is passive. A passive person can control by saying and doing nothing.

Often husbands and fathers fail to see the hearts of their spouses and their children. They are busy making ends meet and keeping the wheels of productivity turning, getting the job done, giving orders.

Such fathers overlook the importance of relating, of talking, of actively caring about feelings. Then mothers tend to overdo trying to balance the emotional budget.

Are you spoiling your children by over-indulgence or harshness?

"Our fathers disciplined us for a while as they thought best; but God disciplines us for our good, that we may share in his holiness" (Hebrews 12:10).

THE GOVERNOR AND CAESAR'S GRANDDAUGHTER

CLAUDIA PROCULA AND PONTIUS PILATE

Pilate's wife is not named in Scripture, but historians tell us that she was Claudia Procula, granddaughter of Augustus Caesar. Because of her influence over Sejanus, Caesar's counselor, Claudia was allowed to accompany her husband to his political assignment as governor of Judea.

Whether Pilate was equally open to Claudia's desires is not clear. When Claudia "suffered a great deal" in a dream about Jesus, just before He was brought to Pilate for trial, she felt free enough with Pilate to write him a note interceding for Jesus. Pilate, however, ignored her attempt at intervention, washing his hands in a dramatic display of neutrality.

Was Pilate embarrassed by his wife's effort to influence his decision in matters of state, especially in the presence of scoffing Jewish leaders who would never have allowed such interference by *their* wives? Was he simply annoyed by his Roman wife's interest in a lowly Jew? Whatever the case, he washed his hands of the whole mess.

Pilate was transferred out of Judea a short time later. The rest of Claudia and Pilate's story is never told, as though Pilate's hands had washed the slate of history as well.

Bible Background: Matthew 27:15–26.

113

CLAUDIA PROCULA

INTIMACY AND IMPORTANCE

He's innocent!
I'm sure of it!" she said.

But how to persuade Pilate?

He'll think my dream a vapor,
   a nightmare that will
            disappear in day.
My husband is a *very*
            important man.

How does a wife
   get her very important man
      to listen to her
   when her convictions seem
      very unimportant
      very impractical
      very unrelated to the real
         world?

Conviction made
            compromise
            unthinkable.
   She pled Christ's innocence
      and went down in history
         as a woman
      who did all she could.

When God created men and women in His own image, He seems to have differentiated important aspects of His own nature. Then He tells us to be one again.

Both men and women portray some important truth about God, who contains within Himself all nonphysical aspects of maleness and femaleness. God dwells with angels in the heavens, but longs for intimacy with us, dwelling inside hearts.

"Being one" is making space in your mind and heart, giving respectful consideration for everything the other believes important.

When your spouse speaks, God may be trying to tell you something. Are you listening?

"Submit to one another out of reverence for Christ" (Ephesians 5:21).

PONTIUS PILATE

WINNING BY LOSING

He washed his hands.

Christ's innocence
  was not important to
    Pilate—
      only his own popularity.
Claudia's convictions
  were not important to
    Pilate—
      only his need to please
        the people.
Pilate's conscience
  was not important to
    Pilate—
      only his own ambition.

How important is
  "looking good"
    plying power
      climbing the corporate
        ladder
        to me?

Power and popularity create their own special delusions. The hunger for them often comes from deep wells of insecurity and is fed by subservience or applause.

The powerful person can create victims. The popular person is often himself the victim of the need to please people.

God is all-powerful, yet He chooses to forgo the exercise of that power so that He can love—and save—everyone, anyone, on either side of the human power struggle. He went all the way over to the side of weakness—and died—to show the power of love.

Have you ever tried to win by losing?

"Your attitude should be the same as that of Christ Jesus: Who being in very nature God, did not consider equality with God something to be grasped, but made himself nothing, taking the very nature of a servant, being made in human likeness" (Philippians 2:5–7).

115

THE FACTOR OF FLEXIBILITY

MR. AND MRS. PETER

She married a fisherman—but most of their married life was spent "fishing for men."

She had a mother who may have become her sole support when the fisherman-husband left home to fish for men—but this mother became very ill. Peter's lonely wife may have wondered why the Master took everyone from her.

And then the Master restored her mother's health, and Mrs. Peter realized that the Master never takes without His giving back.

How did Peter's wife feel when she heard that her husband had denied Jesus? Apprehensive, ashamed, grieved? Did she find it hard to forgive him?

Later in life, Peter's wife accompanied her husband on his missionary journeys. That probably required even more flexibility than managing a home alone!

An old church tradition tells that Peter and his wife died together (also that he was crucified upside down) and that he comforted her with these words: "Remember the Lord." Evidently the faith of Peter's wife was as strong as his own renewed faith.

Bible Background: Matthew 8:14–15 26:69–75, John 21:1–25, 1 Corinthians 9:5.

117

PETER

MARRIAGE IS MINISTRY

Lord, when I think of Peter
I think of myself
  impulsive
  speaking before I think
  denying You, Lord, so
    many times
  saying by my actions if
    not my voice
  "I don't know Him!"
  "I don't know Him!"
  "I don't know Him!"

Is that why You asked Peter,
    three times:
  "Lovest thou Me?"
  "Lovest thou Me?"
  "Lovest thou Me?"

Lord, You know all things.
  You know I love You.
    Please teach me
      to feed Your sheep.
  You want me to begin
    by nourishing her
    cherishing her
    leading her by still
      waters
      as unto You?

And she is not even one of
    the least of these . . . .

Ministry sometimes hurts marriage because the marriage is not viewed as ministry too. There's a lot of witnessing to be done inside the family.

Christian marriage is meant to demonstrate to the world Christ's sacrificial, patient, tender love for people who are not always nice or lovable. That is very hard to do! What an object lesson!

People's greatest needs and hurts are inside their families. People want to hear and see a gospel that works inside families.

Is your marriage witnessing like that?

———————

"May they be brought to complete unity to let the world know that you sent me and have loved them even as you have loved me" (John 17:23b).

MRS. PETER

CHANGES

After all those years of
staying home
  with the kids (if they had
      some)
  it must have been quite a
      change
    for Peter's wife
      to start traveling with
      her husband.

Was he considerate of her
      travel needs
  her longing for privacy
      and time alone
  her emotional and
      physical exhaustion
  her yearning for the Sea
      of Galilee and home?

Knowing Peter, probably not,
    at least at first.
    Perhaps he learned in
      time.
It's good his wife had learned
      patience
  years earlier.

On days when all I can see
  are trials and tribulations,
    remind me, Lord,
  that testing develops
      patience
  and that I'm just
      in training.

Your spouse may be a traveling sales-
man, an evangelist, in the service—
whatever the occupation, he's away
from home most of the time. You think
the days of doing it all yourself, caring
for the children alone, will never end.

And then, before you know it, the nest
is empty. There's too much time on
your hands. Aloneness becomes as trou-
bling as the tension of togetherness
once was. The children are gone!

Adjustments and changes, however
welcomed, create lots of stress and oft-
hidden anxiety.

Are you talking about all these feelings and fears openly and honestly with
your spouse?

---

*"Consider it pure joy . . . whenever you
face trials of many kinds, because you
know that the testing of your faith
develops perseverance. Perseverance must
finish its work so that you may be mature
and complete, not lacking anything"*
(James 1:2–4).

A MATTER OF
CHOICE

ANANIAS AND SAPPHIRA

It was their choice, no one else's. They had not been forced into the agreement. As members of the New Testament church, they had made the promise to share all that they had with other members of the early Christian community.

The problem came when they brought only a part of the money they had been paid for a piece of property, claiming it was the full price. Selfishly, they wanted to be praised for their unselfishness.

But the Holy Spirit revealed Ananias's deceptiveness to the Apostle Peter. He confronted Ananias with the truth; Ananias had also lied to the Holy Spirit. His heart and spirit failed him when he realized that his secret ambition had become public knowledge. He dropped dead.

Several hours later, Sapphira revealed that she was a collaborator in crime. "How could you agree to test the Spirit of the Lord?" Peter asked. "Look! The feet of the men who buried your husband are at the door, and they will carry you out also."

And great fear seized the whole church and all those who heard.

Like Peter and his wife, this couple died together—but how differently! One couple gave all, with no regrets; the other couple tried to hold back part of what they had promised to God, and lost everything.

Bible Background: Acts 5:1–11.

121

ANANIAS

Barnabas is a good man!"
"He's spirit-filled. . . ."
"Barnabas is a man of faith."
"He's such an encourager!"

Did it seem to Ananias
  that someone else
    —perhaps Barnabas—
      was always one step
        ahead?
  that someone else always
      took credit
    for *his* innovative ideas?
  that someone else always
      got the applause
  when *he* deserved it?

Just this once,
  did Ananias say,
    just this once
      I'll be the hero!
      I just won't tell the
        whole truth.
        They don't need to
        know everything.

How awful! Two people struck dead for merely hiding part of the truth!

There are many dead marriages today, dressed up in Sunday clothes and laid out for display, like perfect corpses in polished coffins—and viewers say, "Don't they look wonderful?"

People who look OK on the outside are often dying inside, victims of nameless infections that could be healed if they were brought to light.

Your marriage, no matter how good or bad it now is, can have a resurrection to new life!

Will you humbly share your struggles with caring friends?

"On the outside you appear to people as righteous, but on the inside you are full of hypocrisy and wickedness" (Matthew 23:28).

122

SAPPHIRA

COMPLIANCE OR INTEGRITY?

Perhaps power and
possessions
   were important to Sapphira.

Did she care more
  about what she had
    than what she was?

Was she more interested
  in what people thought
    than in what God knew?

Did she choose honor over
    honesty?
      importance over
      integrity?
Or was she simply too
    submissive
  to a husband
    who didn't know how
      to submit to God?

How much compliance, how much submission is appropriate if your spouse is involved in sinful or unwise practices? Must you refrain from good things if your spouse objects?

Your submission is "as unto the Lord." Jesus could deny Himself His rights and comforts, but He would never do wrong or deprive another person.

Saying no in a loving way to your spouse's wrongdoing or selfishness, and demonstrating the beauty of holiness in your own patient attitude, is surely right, although never easy.

Who is right does not matter; what is right is very important.

Will you pray together in order to understand God's will?

"And whatever you do, whether in word or deed, do it all in the name of the Lord Jesus, giving thanks to God the Father through him" (Colossians 3:17).

A TRIO OF TENTMAKERS
PRISCILLA AND AQUILA

When the Emperor Claudius expelled all Jews from Rome, a Jewish couple named Priscilla and Aquila boarded a ship headed for Corinth. Corinth was a haven for seafarers, a resort for wealthy Athenian businessmen and the home of the famous temple of Aphrodite, the Greek goddess of love, served by a thousand priestess-prostitutes.

In this pleasure-seeking environment, the two humble tentmakers met a man of like trade, recently emigrated from Athens—Paul, who told them of Jesus the Christ. And they believed.

So ardently did they believe that they followed Paul to Ephesus and established a church there in their home. Priscilla, whose name is placed before Aquila's in three out of five instances—an unusual honor for a woman of those days—worked with her husband in teaching the learned and eloquent Apollos the way of God.

Opposition and persecution were inevitable, since Ephesus housed one of the Seven Wonders of the World, the Temple of Diana. At least once Priscilla and Aquila risked their lives for Paul.

Their names go down in history as a couple who gave their all—to each other, to their friends and to their God.

Bible Background: Acts 18:1–3, 24–26.

125

AQUILA

HUMBLE

He had to give up
everything
    —a tiny shop, perhaps, in
        Rome
    a plot of land
    a little home
encourage his wife
    move to a new place
    and begin again.

Their new home was in
        Corinth,
    a sailor's paradise—
        wine on every street
        prostitutes on every
            corner.
Aquila's eyes saw Paul.

They followed Paul to
        Ephesus
    where all the world came
        to see the temple of Diana
        and worship her.
Aquila's eyes saw Jesus.

A humble tentmaker
    never looking back at what
        he'd lost
    or looking for the past
    always looking forward
    greeting a new day
        with determination and
            courage

ready to give up anything
ready to move anywhere
ready to be God's man.

The companionship of a "we" relationship, the unity and harmony that make teamwork possible and productive is beautiful to behold.

Marriage is not meant for two people to simply enjoy each other. Marriage has many tasks. Tasks require work and serving one another and enabling each other to serve others.

Of course mutual servanthood also produces pleasures and joys, but the couple—and family—that intentionally participates in some cause larger than themselves view each other with increasing respect and reverence.

Do you see needs beyond your own and gladly serve others, as well as your own family?

"Rather, serve one another in love"
(Galatians 5:13b).

PRISCILLA

GIFTED

How I admire Priscilla,
  a woman whose flexibility
    made her priceless!
From Rome to Corinth to
      Ephesus
  she faithfully accompanied
      her husband
    using her skill as a
      tentmaker
      to gain new
        opportunities
        for witness.
Her name precedes her
      husband's
  in some scriptural
      accounts—
    a sign of great respect
      for her ability.
  She taught Apollos well
    about the ways of God.

Teach me to be flexible, Lord
  when my feet want to stay
but my heart knows
    it is time to move on.

God wanted Adam to have a helper suitable for him. Helping implies that two people have the same goal and tasks that move in that direction. Priscilla and Aquila were a team like that—they worked well together.

In Genesis man and woman had identical role assignments. Both were told by God to replenish the earth and have dominion.

Only after they sinned did the pain of separate roles begin—the controversies of headship and submission.

In Christ, oneness is restored, the blessedness of togetherness!

Is any sin or selfishness or exclusiveness spoiling your cooperation in God's plan for you?

"God blessed them and said to them, 'Be fruitful and increase in number; fill the earth and subdue it. Rule over . . . every living creature that moves on the ground' " (Genesis 1:28).

A COUPLE
WHO DESERVED
EACH OTHER

FELIX AND DRUSILLA

The historian Tacitus said of Felix, governor of Judea, "He held the power of a tyrant with the disposition of a slave"——an unprincipled, rebellious one, we can assume.

Felix crushed a movement led by an Egyptian false prophet. He also lured his third wife, Drusilla, away from her first husband with a hired magician.

The governor eliminated bands of robbers and thwarted organized assassins, but he was recalled by Rome after six years of misrule in a corrupt administration.

Felix wrote his own rules for life.

When Paul was brought to trial for "stirring up riots among the Jews," Felix listened to Paul speak of faith and talked with Paul frequently. But when Paul spoke of judgment, the governor was afraid. When Felix was called to Rome, he left Paul in prison.

Drusilla had deserted her first husband for Felix. Felix deserted his first two wives—and Paul. How long do you suppose Felix and Drusilla's "love" lasted?

Bible Background: Acts 24:1–27.

129

FELIX

Felix knew the story
  but he missed the message.
He was "well acquainted
      with the Way"
  but he closed his ears
    before the truth
      could penetrate his
      heart.
He listened to Paul speak
  of righteousness
    self-control
      and judgment to come
  but guilt closed the door to
      life.
    His administration was
      corrupt.
    He'd lured his wife
      away from her first
      husband
      with a hired magician.
    He had much to fear
      from judgment.

"Enough for now!" he said.
  "I'll send for you again . . .
    when it's convenient."

An unbelieving husband, prominent in world affairs, this Felix—yet he carried inside a hungry heart. Hungry hearts yearn for what only God Himself can satisfy, through right relationships and worthwhile work.

But Felix was timid, weak and vacillating. Perhaps he thought he could put off such a life-changing decision until he made more money or achieved some earthly goal. Or perhaps he heard Paul only to satisfy his beautiful young wife's curiosity.

In any case, he chose to hang on to the things that would perish and let go of the rich potential of the eternal.

Would any wise or sane man make such a decision? Would you?

"A man who commits adultery lacks judgment; whoever does so destroys himself. Blows and disgrace are his lot, and his shame will never be wiped away" (Proverbs 6:32–33).

130

DRUSILLA

INSTABILITY

Drusilla—a strange name
and a strange life!
A Jewess married at fifteen
to a heathen king,
several years later
living with a governor,
exiting marriage and
Scripture
as quickly as she
entered—
like people I have met
drifting in, then out
of my life.

Do I make a difference in
their lives
or do they wander on
as aimlessly as before?

Perhaps I need to ask . . .
have I let Jesus make a
difference
in my life
and in our marriage?
Do I see marriage as a
lifelong commitment
that gives the ones who
watch
a living example
of Christ's love for
them?

Was it "too much, too soon" for Drusilla? The headlong rush into adult experiences may create a giddy, flighty frame of mind . . . or a confused, undependable character . . . or a spoiled, demanding tyrant.

Like her husband, this beautiful young Jewess was probably deeply dissatisfied with life . . . but, brushing Paul's words off just as carelessly as she had walked away from her first marriage, she walked away from God's tender mercy as well.

Are you listening carefully to the cautioning words of Christian friends? God Himself may be speaking to you.

"For the lips of an adulteress drip honey, and her speech is smoother than oil; but in the end she is bitter as gall, sharp as a double-edged sword. Her feet go down to death; her steps lead straight to the grave. She gives no thought to the way of life; her paths are crooked, but she knows it not" (Proverbs 5:3–6).

131

CAUGHT IN THE ACT
A SINFUL WOMAN AND JESUS

The teachers of the law had dragged her from the seclusion of a bedroom to the merciless exposure of the temple courts. Jewish law required witnesses, not just compromising evidence, and she had been "caught in the act."

In the process of bringing her to this mock trial, however, the other participant in the drama had been lost or, more probably, ignored—even though anyone knows that adultery cannot be committed alone.

"In the Law Moses commanded us to stone such women," the teachers said. But they were misquoting Moses' directions in Leviticus 20:10: "If a man commits adultery with another man's wife—with the wife of his neighbor—both the adulterer and the adulteress must be put to death."

The trap intended for Jesus closed tightly around the teachers of the Law as the Giver of all good laws pronounced the verdict: "If any of you is without sin, let him be the first to throw a stone at her."

Sandals bit the dust as would-be stonethrowers reluctantly turned away from their disheveled target, convicted by their own guilt. Soon only Jesus was left with the woman.

He did not condone her actions or condemn her broken spirit. He released her from man's inhumanity to womanhood with freeing words: "Neither do I condemn you. Go . . . leave your life of sin."

Bible Background: John 8:1–11.

133

A SINFUL WOMAN

FORGIVEN

Eyes of interest
  eyes of lust
    eyes of scorn
      eyes of mistrust—
I've seen them all
  but never before
    have I been known
      by eyes of love.

Eyes of hatred
  and disbelief
    have called me harlot
      and whore and thief.

These eyes are different.
  They're set apart.
    They see my soul.
      They know my heart.
I can confess
  the nights of sin
    when eyes of love
      bring light within.

These eyes pierce through
  the muck, the dirt.
    They promise healing
      for all the hurt.

Who was she, this sinful woman? Who is she? Unfaithful wife, faithless mother, child abuser, drug user, always hurting herself, looking for love in all the wrong places—and hurting those she leaves behind. . . .

Is she me? Is she you? Is there any hope for such as we, better sinners and worse saints?

Have you really looked up into the eyes of Jesus, who came to show us what our Father God is like? Did you see what is really there?

"No condemnation," He says. "I forgive you. I understand how you came to this. Now, learn to love yourself the way I love you."

How can we?

"Do not be afraid; you will not suffer shame. Do not fear disgrace; you will not be humiliated. You will forget the shame of your youth and remember no more the reproach of your widowhood" (Isaiah 54:4).

134

JESUS

THE PERFECT LOVER

In awe
I bow low before the Man
    who incarnates
purity and power
patience and passion
    in holy Oneness.

His bridegroom love is
    fresh as the morning dew
    unfailing in its ministry
        to each blade of grass
awesome as the summer
        thunder
    rending the blue with its
        power
unceasing as the ocean
        waves
    and as impossible to resist
winsome as a sleeping child
    catching me off guard
        with its unexpected
        tenderness
persistent as the gentle rain
    probing into the desert of
    my soul.

His bridegroom love
        continually bathes
        the Bride
    —a daily washing by the
        Word—
cleansing her wounds with
        His forgiveness

comforting her weakness with His
    strength
caressing her spirit with His peace.

Oh, may I love as He loves,
    this Bridegroom of my soul.

Jesus, on earth, whose perfect love, compassion and understanding, without marriage or sex, attracted and held the utmost devotion of all kinds of women who became His loyal followers.

Jesus, the God-Husband, who goes on loving us and bringing us back to Himself no matter how far away we stray, no matter how deplorable we have become.

Jesus, the Man who sees all the way through who we are . . . to who we can be, because of *love!*

Jesus, ever-alive, to be the Perfect Lover for us all! The Bridegroom waiting to marry me!

Say yes to His proposal!

" 'For your Maker is your husband—the Lord Almighty is his name—the Holy One of Israel is your Redeemer; he is called the God of all the earth. The Lord will call you back as if you were a wife deserted and distressed in spirit—a wife who married young, only to be rejected,' says your God" (Isaiah 54:5–6).

135

Other books by Joy Jacobs include

They Were Women, Too and

When God Seems Far Away.

To order these books or additional copies of

One I Love, contact your local Christian bookstore

or call Christian Publications toll-free

1-800-233-4443.